THE
MONK'S CHOICE

Stories on a path of wisdom

BY

DAVID McARTHUR

Books by David McArthur
The Intelligent Heart
Your Spiritual Heart
The Monk's Choice

Paperback ISBN: 978-1-64184-579-3
eBook ISBN: 978-1-64184-580-9

Published by Tom Bird Retreats, Inc. with AccessingWisdom.com
19857 Whispering Willow Pl NE Unit 100 Poulsbo, WA 98370
info@accessingwisdom.com https://accessingwisdom.com

"Between stimulus and response there is a space.
In that space is our power to choose our response.
In our response lies our growth and our freedom."
Viktor E. Frankl

DEDICATION

This book is dedicated to the monks who raised me,
my parents, Bruce and Charlotte McArthur

CONTENTS

PART II - LIVING

PART 2A - LONG AGO ~ MEILIN ~

PART 2B - TODAY

FORWARD

If there were ever a crucial time for humanity to access the wisdom of their hearts, that time is now. David McArthur is a man worth knowing. If you can't know him in person, then meet his integrity of character, his kindness, compassion and wisdom through his books. This newest book, *The Monk's Choice*, is, in my estimation, his best yet. It's as though it was written to offer hope for the emotional tenor of this age of pandemic, financial and political upheaval and climate change. Yet I know David began this book well before the inner and outer climates of humanity reached these current levels of uncertainty.

Happily, I've been a close friend of David and his family as well as a colleague of David's for nearly three decades. David is a master storyteller. He expresses his abiding care for humanity through the stories he tells, which have levels of depth that will warrant re-reading—for enjoyment and to feel the emotional uplift that he offers. You will experience his heart as you read his books but more importantly, you will be inspired to follow your own heart's awakening to another level of compassion, kindness and love. Knowing David as I do, that would be his heart's desire for you as you read his book. What greater gift can we give to each other?

Here's why I encourage you to read this book: the storyline is replete with ancient, archetypal wisdom that beacons us to a higher place within. And that place consistently points to the essence of who we are. Why does that matter? In my experience, humanity's very essence, our nature as whole beings living on a planet in chaos, is to change, flex, question old perceptions and remember that we are here to Be Love. We all need inspiration and reminders that we *really do* want to live the way of love through our hearts—even if that sometimes seems like an impossible dream. This book will inspire and remind you. Like the monks, when we expand to meet our awakening hearts, we become freer to be who we truly are, rather than be imprisoned in the automatic firing of old neural circuitry, wondering why it's so hard to think our way into compassion or kindness. It's not hard; it's impossible. It's not an intellectual process to live in a state of love and compassion.

David engages you in the monk's journey to take you beyond words and into the language of the heart. It's a familiar language because the telling of this story touches what is unspoken, beautiful yet deeply known within in all of us: the wisdom of our hearts. As you read this lovely book, surrender to the levels of experience that are offered to you, reading the lines and between the lines. You are highly likely to rediscover aspects of yourself there. That's the genius of David's story: it makes what is indescribable, real. Thousands of people all over the world have enjoyed and loved David as a minister, as a friend, as an author and speaker. He knows the full territory of his own heart and therefore, he can speak to yours.

I invite you to read this book as though it was written especially for you. David knows that in the heart we are not separate. That is the essential message of this wonderful book, and it's a message that could not be timelier. Put your feet up, dive into this book and dive into your heart. You will be so glad you did.

Toni Roberts

INTRODUCTION

I was probably eleven or twelve when I first heard the story of the monk. I found it inspiring, and I wanted to be able to make choices like the monk. I wanted the skill to be at peace in my inner world. I wanted to be in compassion when others were afraid. I wanted the skill to feel the beauty of life in the storm as well as in the sunshine. I wanted to see the beauty around me in the nighttime as well as in daylight. I longed for the profound wisdom that comes from the choice the monk made.

However, it was many years after first hearing of the monk that I understood how valuable the monk's choice really is. Events early in my life (which I shared in my earlier book, *Your Spiritual Heart*) helped me understand that the monk's choice was possible. It was then, when life let me experience the alternate choices we make, that I seriously began to seek the skill to make the monk's choice at will. I was eager to discover if the monk's tale, and the choice it spoke of, was really possible in today's world.

Could we as humans actually respond to life's experiences of hurt or fear as the monk did? Do we really have a deeper level of profound wisdom within us, as the monk possessed?

I began to search for that answer.

It was when I came across some breakthrough scientific research that I began to understand the true nature of the monk's choice. This research makes it clear not just how to activate this inner transformation but also how to access our deeper wisdom.

There are two parts to this book, each built around a story of a monk bringing his or her gifts to a village. Each part begins with a tale of a monk from long ago, followed by real people in today's world applying the skills taught in the tale. I have included the science and some of the spiritual understandings of the dynamic taking place in these transformations. The two parts combine to offer what I have found to be a very simple yet powerful set of practices to connect with our hearts and experience the transformation and wisdom that comes from doing so.

I hope this simple writing captures the transformative message of the monks' tales for you, as the stories captured it for me. I have taken the liberty to flesh out the stories as I imagined them to have happened. I hope you find, as many people in addition to myself have found, that the monk's choice can be just as much a reality in today's life as it was ages ago.

I want to offer a special acknowledgment to the people at the HeartMath® Institute, whose research and techniques have taught our contemporary world how to make the powerful choices this book reveals. They have given me special permission to share with you The Heart Wisdom Tool, which is my adaptation of their technique, Freeze-Frame®. Their understanding of our heart's intelligence and the impact of the choices I am sharing with you here is exceptional and deeply appreciated.

The monk's choice is a real choice. Test it out. Experience how it can work for you.

From my heart,
David McArthur

PART I

CHOOSING

PART 1A
LONG AGO

~ MING'S CHOICE ~

CHAPTER 1
VILLAGE OF FEAR

The growing roar of the stream alongside the trail gradually overwhelmed the rhythmic thump of his staff striking the ground. As the water cascaded down the steep mountainside, its cool mist created occasional patches of silver luminescence in the early-morning light. With the determined footfall of one who traverses great distances, the monk walked steadily upward.

The trail continued its ascent away from the stream, through the dark green of scattered trees and grassy meadows, where the blue and yellow of the last spring wildflowers brought a smile to the monk's worn features.

By midmorning, he topped a ridge where the dark red stone reflected the dryer, harsher climate of the valley before him.

The monk looked up at the craggy rocks of a mountain plateau where, he had heard, there was a simple village, a village he had sought for days.

The monk was not sure why he was going to that remote mountain village. It had just felt right to head in that direction when he heard it mentioned. He liked out-of-the-way places. This village, high in the rugged mountains, was indeed out of the way.

The monk had left the well-traveled roads behind the day before. He had passed the last small gathering of mud-colored huts that could be called a village yesterday.

The monk smiled at his choice as he felt a gentle surge of joy in his heart. To let himself be led through the countryside by simply feeling a place call to his heart would have been very strange for him at an earlier time in his life. There was no outer reason, no goal or need expressed for this journey. Yet, after years of learning to recognize and follow his heart's direction, he knew there would be purpose and meaning in this journey. Even if he could not anticipate what it would be.

The monk's name was Ming. Ming had been living the life of a monk for many years. As a monk he had traveled to many villages, large and small. He had come to enjoy these journeys into the remote countryside to places and people he did not know.

For days he had wandered along broad quiet rivers, then beside the smaller streams with the sound of their turbulence almost drowning out the birdsong that filled forest and meadow. From there he had ascended up into the dark-green foliage of the foothills. The road he traveled led him to this path that had diverged from the noise and moisture of the mountain stream. Ming stood on the stony ridge from which he could look up at the distant mountain plateau where he believed the village to be. He could see on the mountainside above the plateau a few spots of green where crops might be cultivated.

The bushes along his path to the plateau became increasingly stunted. The greener grass of the valleys gave way to the hardy, coarse, mountain grass in the meadows he glimpsed through the trees.

As Ming looked upward at the precipitous edge of the plateau, he guessed that the people of the village would be herders. They were probably farmers who raised sheep and goats on the scruffy forage. The path before him, although narrow, was worn deep, as if the village had existed in this remote corner of the mountains for a very long time.

Ming liked herding villages. He had been raised in one. It had been a simple life. It wasn't easy, though, because everything was about caring for the animals and their needs through the changing seasons.

The village in which he had been raised had been a wonderful place to grow up. At a young age, his father would take him on the morning trek to the meadows where the goats and sheep grazed.

He remembered the fun he had with the other children early in the morning, as the herders filled the troughs with water from the town's well. It was a time of games, contests, and dares as the children played together. Ming loved trying to outrace the other boys. Then his father would call and together they would move their herd away from the drinking troughs and out to the hillsides where the animals would graze.

Those memories brought a smile to his face and a glow to his heart. That carefree play of childhood was indeed a very special moment in his life. He looked forward to tomorrow's early morning at the well in the village before him. He would be able to watch children play and listen to men talk about their animals and the weather.

The monk crested a rise; suddenly the village was displayed before him. There were the rails of the pens and beyond them several dozen mud houses, the same dusty ocher color as the earth around them. The spaces of packed dirt between them were darker, hardened by many feet, young and old, over many years. The dark-green foliage of gnarled ancient trees spread throughout the village, giving it a soft, inviting feel. Ming felt the inner pull of the beauty of such simplicity.

Ming had known the houses of those who were rich and those who were powerful. He had seen the beautiful things that come with wealth, and there had been a time when he thought he wanted that. Indeed, there had been a time when money, power, and the things they bought had been his. Now, as he was nearing this small remote village, it was its simplicity that beckoned him.

As he approached the village, Ming heard the bleating of goats and noticed that some of the animals were still in the pens at this late-morning hour. This was strange. The herders he knew would have moved their sheep and goats out into their daytime pastures by now. As he neared the houses, he could see the village square ahead and indeed there were children playing at its edge. Their laughter lifted his spirits and he found himself laughing as some young boys suddenly swept by him in a fast-paced game of tag.

He saw the colorful clothing of a group of women near the square. However, they were off to the side instead of at the well where they would normally gather to draw water and visit while the children played. Then he saw a gathering of men by the well. There seemed to be tension in their movements and some voices were raised. Hearing the strident voices, Ming touched his heart and gently sent his breath in and out through his heart. The feeling of calm he had come to know would be there gently enveloped him.

Even though he was a stranger, everyone was so preoccupied in their conversations, with many voices raised and hands gesticulating wildly, that they did not seem to notice the monk as he calmly made his way to a stone bench near the well. He took a seat and turned his attention to what the men were saying.

He soon understood that the villagers had discovered just that morning that their well was dry. He heard the fear in their voices as this simple situation beyond their control threatened the very existence of their town — and perhaps their lives.

CHAPTER 2
MORNING AT THE WELL

As always, Jain had awakened that morning just before dawn. He rose from his bed quietly, trying not to disturb his wife. Crossing the dirt floor, he knelt down by the sleeping boy, whose dark curly hair was almost covered by the coarse wool blanket, and touched his shoulder. The boy stirred, then those bright eyes that so delighted his father popped open. With a smile he nodded his head. Yes, he was coming. The two dressed quickly and quietly in the darkness and headed out into the cool early-morning air toward the pens where their goats awaited. The boy, Shen, was proud that he and his father were always the first to water their flock in the morning. He felt so grown-up now that his father was including him in the morning ritual of caring for their flock. Sometimes, his father would allow him to accompany them into the fields where the animals would graze the mountain grasses under their watchful eyes. He was among the youngest of the boys who were allowed to accompany the flocks. This gave him great stature among the children who would shortly be gathering at the town well. Because he and his father watered their goats first, he would be the first at the well just as the dawn would start to lighten the sky.

The goats were easy to move to the well. This was a familiar routine, and they were bleating and jostling each other in their eagerness for their morning drink. As the goats approached the troughs that extended out from the well, Jain strode forward to lower the heavy bucket on the structure that supported it. Today, both man and boy turned suddenly and stared at the well. Instead of the familiar splash of the bucket striking the water, they head a dull thump. Shen looked with concern at his father. Even as young as he was, Shen knew this was not the right sound. This was not the sound that had been greeting him since his first days of their morning ritual.

Shen saw the sudden worry on his father's face. Jain reached out and pulled on the thick rope that held the bucket. He did not even bother with the crank. He lifted the rope and then let it go. Again, the only sound was the dull thud of the bucket striking ground instead of water.

Again and again, Jain lifted the bucket and let it drop. It was as though he would awaken from a nightmare and the water he so desperately needed for his family and flock would be there. His face mapped his journey from incredulity to anguished acceptance.

Shen watched silently, knowing not to ask, only to hope. The goats increased their bleating, as the water they expected did not come forth.

"What is it, Father? Why is there no water?" Shen finally had to ask.

In a voice that felt heavy to hear, Jain responded, "The well is dry. There is no water here."

Turning from the well, Jain wanted to smile to Shen to make him feel all right, but he could not. It wasn't all right. It was catastrophic. With no water they would have to leave. Their days in this town, one of the few towns Jain had ever been to, were over.

Jain finally became aware of the goats bleating and said to Shen, "Let's take them back to the pens. Others will be coming, and we will have to figure out what to do." The animals were less easy to work with on the way back to the pens. They had not had their water and did not want to leave the place where they knew their water should be. Jain felt the same way. "I don't want to leave," he told himself, knowing that he would have no choice.

Jain felt anger welling up within him. How could this happen? How could the well have changed so much and they did not know the water was disappearing? It did not make sense to him. In the faint early-morning light, Jain turned and watched his neighbor's sheep approach. He heard his friend's voice calling greeting and suddenly felt desperate. His thoughts became more and more frantic. He was searching in his mind for a reason. With a feeling of anger, he began asking himself, "Who has done this?"

Jain's friend's sheep came trotting noisily up to the trough where there would be no water to greet them. He spotted Jain standing by the well and waved. Jain did not wave back.

As Jain's fellow herdsman approached the well, he was able to see the dark frown on Jain's face. He hurried over to his friend even as the sounds of the flocks of other herders could be heard in the distance. As he reached Jain, his friend's look of despair made his stomach tighten. Even though he anticipated some problem, he was not prepared for the terrible news Jain's voice carried.

"The well is dry."

The simple words stopped him short. "No!" He took the two steps to the well and grabbed the bucket. He lowered it hand over hand until he heard the dull thud. He lifted the bucket and let it drop again, hearing the same heart-deadening sound.

Finally, he turned back to Jain. "What do we do? How could this happen?" His anger rose as the desperation of their plight dawned on him. "Someone must have done something to anger the Spirits. We must find them and set this right."

The village was beginning to stir. The early yellow and quiet blue of the dawn had already lightened the sky and other voices could be heard as more herders began the morning ritual of caring for their flocks. These men, used to the hardship of dealing with nature in the form of weather and predators, had never considered they may have to take their families and their flocks and leave this village where many of them had lived all their lives.

As they approached and learned the tragic news, each one exclaimed in denial, grabbed the bucket, and listened to the dull thud of its wood hitting the ground. Soon someone had taken a torch, descended into the well, and then been hauled up. There was no water. It was dry. Anger and fear filled their voices. Soon the women and the elders heard the commotion and joined the gathering at the well.

Some of the herders left to take their flocks into the hills where they could find small streams and make it through the day.

Jain's wife was drawn by the noise. She soon realized how devastating this news was for their family. This was their home. It was all that they knew. Jain had been to other villages over the years and she had as well, but not often. Where would they go? The village was remote so that the flocks would not have to compete for the grasses that others claimed. Maybe they would have to go far away to an area where there were no other people?

The questions went on and on for everyone. The women drew to the side and shared their fear. Their village was more remote than most. That also meant that the soldiers did not come here to take their sons and husbands away to fight in wars. If they left this village, they might come across soldiers out in the countryside. What would happen?

The questions continued. Even though the mood of the adults was dark, the children found they were free to play. With the adults distracted, they were soon running and laughing, not fully aware of the terrible discovery.

It was into this chaotic atmosphere that the monk crested the edge of the plateau and looked down upon the village in its tranquil setting. Ming observed the houses, the pens, and the trees that brought to him memories of his childhood. As he entered the village and saw the gatherings of people uncharacteristic for this time of day, he realized something had happened.

As he walked through the people toward the well, he seemed to pass unnoticed, so preoccupied were the villagers in their conversations. Quietly he sat on the stone bench near the well and listened.

Soon he heard the story of the discovery that the well was dry. He heard many questions without answers. He heard the many exclamations of "why?" and "how?" He heard the villagers' fear in the volume of the conversations and the frantic tone of their voices.

As the monk listened, he became more still and serene. He had learned that in the midst of the storm it is best to dwell in a quiet place. He found that place within himself.

Turning around, Jain eventually noticed the monk sitting on the bench. He was startled. This stranger had entered their village without anyone being aware. Jain remembered that the first act of connection with a monk was for a villager to offer the visitor a drink of the water. This was a simple ritual for any stranger, but particularly for the occasional visit from a monk, although Jain could not remember the last time a monk had visited their village.

For a moment he felt guilty that he could not offer this stranger a drink. Then he felt angry. Here was another person who would need water. Every drop of water was suddenly precious — there was none to replenish what little they had stored in the jars in their houses. The monk's presence felt like an intrusion. Here was someone to witness them at their most vulnerable and powerless. Someone who needed water, just as they did.

Jain spoke to those around him. "What is a monk doing here? Don't we have enough problems without one of them?"

Several men grunted angrily, startled to realize there was a stranger in their midst. One gave voice to a thought several suddenly felt, "Maybe he is the reason the Spirits have cursed us."

Jain angrily approached the monk. "What are you doing in our village? We have no water. You should be gone. You will get no warm reception here. Be gone!"

The harshness of Jain's words impacted the monk, who found his own anger quickly rising in response. There had been a day when no one would have dared to speak to him like that.

Ming had been a powerful and successful soldier. As he saw the aggressive posture of this man and heard the angry voice directed at him, his hand started to move to his side where his long, sharp knife had once been kept. He felt the tension in his body as it prepared to leap forward, knife in hand, to punish the man who had so disrespected his person. Such a challenge was something he had been trained to meet violently with his full wrath. It was a response he was very good at. A soldier's reaction was still strong and quick within him.

In the instant the monk felt the anger trigger his body's response, he recognized the reaction as a trigger for another kind of training. The monk's hand did move, but its slow, deliberate movement probably went unnoticed by the burly man whose name the monk would later learn was Jain. The monk slowly brought his hand up and touched his heart.

The monk's real movement was one that could not be seen. It was a movement that held in check the quick strike that Ming's hands had once been trained for, a strike that had inflicted pain on many men. It was the movement away from the trained reaction of the warrior he had once been to the conscious choice of a person who now knew the power of choosing how to respond. The harsh strike never showed because the monk made a choice. He made the choice not to respond from his training as a soldier. Instead, he had made the monk's choice, the choice to respond from his heart.

Jain did not know that even though the monk carried no knife, a single blow from that trained hand could have ended his life. He had not thought of such a possibility. He had simply vented his anger as words of rejection to this stranger, this monk, who had appeared at the well on the day it had gone dry.

The monk's choice, the choice of the heart, was a choice that Ming had committed to when he had left the way of the soldier and donned the gray robe of the monk. When he entered monastic life, this choice of the heart had seemed to

Ming like a choice of weakness. However, through his years of making this choice again and again, he had come to learn of its true power. It was a choice he now knew would serve him and certainly it was a choice that in that moment protected Jain in his fear and foolishness from injury or worse.

It was not a choice that had come easily to Ming. The anger of a soldier was an instinct he had learned to direct and channel. It was the heightened and trained focus of the natural reaction that everyone has when threatened. It was a reaction that had helped him succeed in his very dangerous role as a soldier and it had brought him both victory and success.

Admonitions about the power of the heart had seemed like foolishness when Ming first began his training to become a monk.

Ming had been trained in what he thought power was. He had been a successful, skilled, and cunning soldier. His skill had brought him rich reward from those he fought for. He had been welcomed into their houses and sat at their tables enjoying the best food and the finest wine. He had even married one of the daughters of a wealthy merchant and enjoyed the prestige and power that came with both wealth and his skill as a warrior of renown.

His marriage brought an important change into his life, however. Ming began to open his heart to tenderness and feelings of care for his wife, Ting. He found her beauty, her gentleness, and her care for him a strange thing.

Ming had been taken away from his home by soldiers at a young age. Since then he had only lived the soldier's rough life. Now, though, there were beautiful things in his home. There were beautiful rugs on his floors and fine fabric at their windows and on their bed. Now there was someone whose presence became more and more important to Ming as he and Ting shared the experience of creating a home together.

Ting was a wise and caring young woman. She wanted to make a good home for Ming and the family they would have. As she shared thoughts and tenderness with Ming, he found that he appreciated her more and more each day they were together. His home was the one place he did not need to be wary of someone's motive or harsh reactions.

Ting gave birth to a baby boy. They named their son Ling. Ming would later come to recognize that the moment that spoke most to his heart was the moment he first held his precious son in his arms. As he looked at this tiny helpless being, the warrior's heart, which was rich in courage and loyalty, had opened to a greater depth and, instead of a warrior, a loving father stood present in that moment holding little Ling, his son.

The depth of love he experienced as a father had impacted him with a power he had not known before. He would later realize that his heart connection with that beautiful child would begin the journey that would show him a different life. At that moment, it was simply a flood of emotions that seemed to awaken him to feeling more alive than he had ever known. The short time he spent at home with his wife and son seemed to exist outside of time and space in a dimension that he could reach only in moments of sincere seeking.

In his later world as a monk, he knew how to reach into that special world in his memory. Ming knew that the power he had experienced with his son was very real and not to be discounted in times of conflict.

In the village, as Ming's hand rose to touch his heart, he looked up at the man before him whose words had triggered first anger, then choice within him. He took a long breath, imagining moving the air as a flow of energy through his heart. With his focus now on his heart he recalled the moment he entered the town, when the laughing boys had run across his path in their game of tag. He recalled the delight his heart had felt at their joy and exuberance. He enjoyed that feeling as its energy flowed into his body, releasing the last of his warrior's tension and opening his inner vision.

The monk now looked at Jain in a way that was startlingly different from when the words of rejection had first been spoken. He did not see an attacker standing before him. He now saw with eyes of compassion. He saw a man who was afraid and powerless, venting his fear because he did not know what else to do. With the gift of understanding now flooding his heart, Ming responded with words of acknowledgement and understanding that flowed freely into his mind.

"Do I hear right, that you have just discovered today that your town's well is dry? That must be a frightening thing to discover."

Jain's face showed surprise at this unanticipated response. He hesitated for a moment and then acknowledged, "Yes, this has never happened before. From before my grandfather's time, this well has always given its water to the people of our village. It has never even slowed its flow before."

"I'm guessing you must be thinking about where you can go to find water for your herds. How hard that must be for your women and children. I saw the boys playing when I entered your village. This seems like a good place to raise a family."

Jain responded with the concern that had been weighing most heavily on his mind. "It will be hard to ask my family to move. One of those boys was my son, Shen. With my children so young, leaving our home is hard and dangerous."

"I enjoyed the fun the boys were having. I am sure these changes must be difficult for you and everyone here."

The monk let his compassion flow from his heart across the village. He felt the anguish and fear of the women nearby. He felt the worry of parents thinking of taking their young children away from a place of security and friendship into an unknown future. He rested for a moment in the feeling of compassion.

As he felt the power of his compassion, he was aware that it did not weaken him. He was sensing with understanding the anguish around him. Yet he was not feeling anguish in himself. His compassion was a force of power and strength flowing through him. It gave him understanding. It was like when he was a boy with the herds. He understood the fear of his sheep when a predator was near; however, he had not felt the fear. He had been alert, vigilant, feeling powerful, ready to protect and care for the sheep that were his charges.

CHAPTER 3
FROM SOLDIER TO MONK

Ming had learned that compassion was the feeling that connected him to the life around him, yet there was no room for compassion in his world as a soldier. His only concern was for his fellow soldiers, and when in battle there was only room for the energy of his anger and aggression.

When Ming held his infant son, his heart had let his love flow into compassion for the helplessness of this little being. His compassion had embraced his wife as he felt her heart's desire to nurture and care for their baby. There was in that moment a connection he had not experienced before. He felt at one with his little family; a tenderness filling his heart that did not feel weak, but strong, a strength he had not known before.

These many years later, compassion was a familiar companion in his life's journey. Even surrounded by the emotional struggle of the villagers as they dealt with their fear about the failure of their well, his compassion meant he did not need to feel fear. Through his compassion, he felt strength in his heart. He understood the villagers' fear. It was a very natural response. And yet, the monk stood quietly in strength beside them.

His journey as a monk had begun years before on a day that Ming learned of enemy soldiers approaching the town of the people he served. He responded when called to fight, because he had an even greater investment in the safety of the town that housed his new family. He had no fear of battle as he prepared to leave his home and fulfill his duty.

Combat had always been exciting for Ming. This was the test of his skill. This was the challenge to his strength and the brilliance of his strategy. This was his chance for fame and renown. He had looked forward to the fighting and had great confidence in his superiority as a warrior. This time, though, he realized that a part of him felt connected to his wife and son. It was a different feeling.

When he faced his foes, Ming focused all of his attention on the army before him and inspired his men as they met the attack and joined in the fierce hand-to-hand battle.

For the first time in battle, Ming was struck in the head and lost consciousness. After the fighting swept by him, he awakened on the battlefield. As he looked around him at the dead, dying, and severely wounded men, his gaze fell on the last soldier he had slain. Ming remembered how easily he had dispatched this enemy.

Suddenly, Ming was not looking at an enemy soldier but at a young boy, just as his son would be in a few years. He saw him not as a man of arms but as a boy barely old enough and strong enough to wield a weapon. As he continued to look around him, this battle-hardened soldier saw the destruction of young men whose lives had ended. The potential of their lives was extinguished. They would no longer know friendship or joy. These young men would not hold their children as he had. Was this the fate of his Ling, his son?

Becoming a father had awakened something within Ming. It was a greater view of the world, of life, and of the part of life he was living. Ming looked at his blood-stained sword and suddenly it was repugnant to him. Was this his life, to slaughter the young men of the world?

Ming found the strength to leave the battlefield and begin the journey back toward the city.

As he approached the ridge that led to the beautiful valley where his family lived, he could tell that an army had passed that way. With growing apprehension, he crested the ridge and looked on what had once been a beautiful valley of fields surrounding the vibrant city that had become his home. What he saw was complete destruction. The fields were burned and the houses destroyed, with smoke still rising from their ruins.

With a heavy heart and fear for his wife and child coursing through him, he ran through the streets to what should have been their home. At last he found their street and the remnants of their house, like the others, a smoldering ruin. There, in the smoke and fire, he found their bodies. His world collapsed around him.

There is no way to describe the pain and sorrow that overwhelmed Ming as he held the lifeless bodies of these two people who were so precious to his heart. Though he had known death and suffering all his life, nothing prepared him for the anguish that filled his being. The strength he had to call upon to make it through those days required a greater struggle than he had ever known.

Ming buried his young wife and little son. He worked with other soldiers who were finding their way to the town and buried all of the town people they could. They listened in pain to the stories of the few survivors.

Filled with anger and pain, Ming returned to the graves of the two people he loved so deeply and sank to the ground.

Something happened in Ming at that place. It was not something that anyone would ever explain. Certainly, it was not something that Ming could ever fully understand.

He looked upon the graves of these two people who were so dear to his heart. As he remembered the destruction of the war that had swept over his own town, his own home, his own treasured son, and the wife he loved, something within him changed.

Ming drew his sword and held it up with a cry that would have struck terror into the enemy who had done this horrible thing. His anger overwhelmed him in a moment of rage that was fierce to behold. Then Ming looked at his sword. He saw the weapon that had ended the lives of his loved ones. He saw the weapon that not long before he had used to slay the young boys that reminded him of his own son. Ming dropped his sword as though it were burning his hand. As it clanged to the ground, Ming fell to the earth beside the grave of his family.

It was a long time before he arose. He then turned from the grave and walked away. The sword lay there on the ground. Ming walked away without his sword, a weaponless soldier.

CHAPTER 4

LEARNING THE MONK'S CHOICE

Ming wandered for many days. Perhaps it was months, or even years. Little is known of when or how he came across the monks whose order he would eventually join. Yet, we do know that at some point he came across the teacher, the wizened monk who would teach him that he had another power within him; a power greater than that he had wielded through his sword. When he came across this teacher he would be told of another choice, a choice that he could freely make – the monk's choice, the choice of his heart.

Ming would later tell others that at first, he did not believe this choice was real. He pretended to follow the old monk's instruction to choose his heart. He would raise his hand to his heart and take the focused breath that seemed to flow through the center of his chest. He would focus his attention there, in the area of his heart. He said that this exercise felt good and he thought that was what the old monk meant by choosing his heart.

One day Ming had touched his heart and taken his breath when the old monk approached him. The monk looked at Ming and started to laugh. Ming was surprised and felt offended. He believed he was following the exercise that would connect him with the greater wisdom and power that flowed through him and all life around him. What was the old monk laughing at?

Feeling compassion for the young man before him who lived in such confusion, the old monk asked him why he was afraid.

"I am not afraid," Ming answered tensely.

"You must be afraid," the old monk responded. "You have come to the door of the greatest treasure in life and you stand at the door, but you will not open it. You will not enter. You are afraid to open the door and enter."

Ming did not understand. "I have done as you instructed. I have touched my heart and sent my breath out and back in through my heart."

"Yes, you have," the old monk declared. "That is the journey to the doorway, and you have done that well. And once you have reached the doorway you still must open it. It will not open by your thinking. It will not open by your breathing. It will not open by your wishing. It will not open by your pretending. It will only open by your feeling. You stand at the door, but you do not feel the love that is the key to the door."

Ming thought about what the old monk said. Days later he approached the old monk again and asked him, "How do I feel this love? You are right. I do not feel. I hear the words, but nothing changes in me. I can feel anger. I can feel despair, but that is all. I cannot feel love."

The old monk touched his heart. His breath was deep and gentle. Then he let his love flow out from his heart. His love brought the beautiful, powerful feeling of compassion flowing through his heart, and that compassion seemed to reach out from him and enfold the young man before him.

"There was a time when you loved," the old monk said. "There was a time when your heart was full. Let me guide you on the path to find those beautiful feelings again. The world around you calls you there."

The old monk had Ming look around. He asked him what color caught his eye. Ming acknowledged the blue of a bird that had just alighted on a limb near them. The old monk asked if he liked the blue of the bird.

Ming answered, "Of course. It is very beautiful."

"When you thought beautiful, just before that thought there was a sudden shift, a shift in what you felt. It was small, but it was not anger, it was not rejection, it was positive. Look at that moment when you saw the color of the bird and just before you said 'beautiful,' you felt something," the old monk said as he began the journey of re-introducing the hardened soldier to the world of feeling.

"When you feel the beautiful blue of the bird, can you feel the very gentle lift of your spirit? Do you feel just a little fuller, a little happier than you were a moment ago?"

Ming paid careful attention to himself and finally said, "Yes, there is a very gentle lift within. I did not feel happy, but I did not feel as unhappy as I did a moment before."

"Do you see the yellow of the flower beneath the tree?" the old monk asked.

"Yes," Ming replied.

"See how beautifully it curls? Do you see its exquisite shape and the way the color flows through its petals?"

After a long time of silence, Ming responded, "Yes, I do. It really is exquisite, isn't it?"

"It is indeed," the old monk responded. "But as beautiful as it is there is something that is even more beautiful. It is a sound. Listen."

Ming listened and they both heard the laughter of children playing a little distance away. There were words and songs, squeals of delight, and joyous laughter. As Ming listened, it became like music in his ears. Slowly it seemed to build, and he felt a gentle touch upon his heart. It was not a physical touch. It was like a gentle melting of the ice and snow in the spring. It grew stronger within him, as when the sun begins to fill the sky with the light of early dawn.

Just like that early light, it began to make a space appear where one could not be seen before. The children's laughter began to fill what had seemed to be a hollow place where Ming's heart had been. It began to fill that space and it was gentle yet beautiful, like the color of the bird and the exquisite curve of the yellow petals of the flower.

The old monk said very quietly, almost so quietly it could not be heard, "Breathe that beautiful feeling. Enjoy it as it fills your heart."

So, Ming did. He let that very strange feeling that the children's laughter had awakened flow in and out through his heart. It felt good. It felt strange, because he had not felt such a feeling in a long, long time. Yet it felt familiar, as if it were a part of him or had been a part of his life at some point.

"Breathe that gentle, beautiful feeling deeply and easily," the old monk whispered. And Ming did.

It was some time before Ming moved or even shifted his attention from the laughter of the children and this feeling in his heart. By then his heart seemed to have filled and a strange peace enveloped him. The old monk was no longer there. But that did not surprise Ming. He simply enjoyed the first peace that he had felt in a very long time.

Each day the old monk would come and point out to Ming something of beauty or an exquisite pattern upon which to appreciate and focus. It was a leaf one day, the curl of a fern another. It was the response of the sheep to their master's voice and the way the baby lambs would bounce in their joy and energy.

Each day, Ming would take time to look around and let his eyes find beauty. He would focus on the gentle lift of energy that accompanied his discovery. He listened for the sounds that he learned to appreciate. The bird calls, the animals, the sounds of the children, or the sound of conversations or laughter. Even the sound of crying held its own beauty. It was like seeing and hearing everything around him for the first time.

There came a day when the old monk invited Ming into another experience. He asked Ming if he would like to know the place where wisdom lives. Ming was startled but sat quietly as the monk instructed.

The old monk invited Ming to remember. He asked Ming to remember a time when his heart had felt truly full. He asked Ming to remember a time when that fullness was so great it had overflowed.

As Ming heard the old monk's words, Ming found his memory filling with the most precious moment of his life. He remembered how his heart had swelled as he held the precious baby, his son. He remembered the beauty of this new life, his amazement at the little body, and the potential he had felt in that moment as his heart filled with love.

His heart was full; he felt filled to overflowing. Then the beautiful picture collapsed into the grotesque image of his precious family slaughtered by the soldiers. With a cry of pain, he turned from the old monk and ran to escape the pain that filled him.

CHAPTER 5

AN ANCIENT WISDOM

Days later, the old monk found Ming working in one of the fields the monks tended. The old monk asked him to follow him and took him to a stream that was nearby. He asked Ming to look into the stream and watch the water until he found the fish.

Ming focused his attention on the water, and he began to distinguish between the colors of the ripples. Then he saw a darker color moving differently than the ripples. He saw its shape and realized it was a fish. He pointed to the fish and the monk told him to keep his focus on the fish. Ming watched the fish for several minutes until it darted out of sight. He told the old monk of its disappearance.

"What do you see now?" the old monk asked. Ming described the colors of the pool without the fish. The old monk asked him to describe what he had seen when the fish was there. "Can you see them both at once?" the old monk asked.

Ming tried and said that he could see them both, but not clearly. His focus was either on the surface water of the stream or on the darker, deeper image created by the fish. If it was on the stream surface, the fish's image was vague. If he focused on the fish's image, the surface waters of the stream seemed to fade into background. "Even if I'm aware of them both, only one is clear," he said.

The old monk had him describe again and again first one image, then another.

Then the old monk said to Ming, "It is time for your bravery to come forth. It is time for you to tell me the two images you saw that filled your heart first with love and then pain."

Ming did as the old monk asked. There beside the stream he told the old monk of his wife and the birth of their child. He told of holding their infant and how his heart had filled. He told the monk of how his love for his wife had blossomed in that moment, how hope had lifted him, and how beautiful his son had looked in those first moments of life.

Then he told of the battle, his injury, seeing the young boys he had slain. He told of finding his way home and the devastation of his village. He told of the horrible moment when he found the bodies of the baby and its mother slain by the soldiers, burnt by the fire.

He told of burying their bodies and helping the few remaining villagers. He acknowledged letting his anger fill him and how he suddenly could no longer hold his sword. He said it seemed to burn his hand as he realized that he was not an instrument of strength and valor but of death and destruction. He told of turning away and wandering until his feet had brought him here, to this place where the monks lived.

After a long silence, the old monk said to Ming, "You were given a great gift. It is not an easy gift and not all people who are given that gift can live with this knowledge.

"You were shown that we are creators. We can create life or death, beauty, or pain. Seeing that truth, you made a choice. You turned away from creating pain and destruction. Some who have been given that gift cannot turn away. They return to the sleep of anger and create as they have been taught. You did not know where you were going or how to get there, but you turned to find another way. That is perhaps the greatest courage the warrior possesses. Now let me show you how, at this point in life, that choice is made."

The old monk shared with Ming the ancient wisdom that has been passed from the old ones to the young for generations. He told him of the choice, of life or death, of head or heart. He told him how, like the images of the stream, he could focus on one, but he could not focus on both.

He revealed to Ming how the lift of his feelings from the beauty of the bird or the laughter of the children was his spirit awakening, flowing into his conscious and being called by his focus on life. He let him see that the memories of pain and death forced the spirit from his being because his spirit was life. Ming recognized that it was the choices he made that activated his spirit within him.

The old monk led Ming to realize that the mind, if not guided by his spirit, looked to validate the hand-me-down ideas others had placed in his mind: the soldiers who trained him, the rich people who hired him. He revealed how those ideas had protected him for a while so his body could survive. Through other's ideas he had learned about the three-dimensional world, the world of things Ming had once believed would make him happy. He showed Ming that it was the moment-by-moment flow of wisdom from his spirit that constantly brought new-ness, care, and potential into each moment. Ming discovered how through his heart he could connect with this spirit for wisdom that provided in each moment what was needed. It provided abundance as well as wisdom, even when only wisdom was sought.

Ming went back to the memory of holding his tiny son in his strong hands. He focused all of his attention on that moment and the feelings of love that had filled his heart. He would not let his mind wander to the pain that had followed. This memory was a pure moment with its own presence and truth and Ming learned to focus on and feel its exquisite beauty and its power.

The months that followed were a time of rich learning for the young man. His view of life changed and filled. He saw the amazing level of choice that presented itself to him each moment. Most importantly, he learned how to make the monk's choice, the choice of his heart.

Ming learned that he could return to the memory of holding his son and re-experience those exquisite feelings of the overwhelming love that flowed through his heart. He learned he could keep his focus on his heart and the head's painful memories faded against the vibrancy and life of his spirit filled with love's power.

Most surprising to Ming was the discovery of his wisdom. He had heard the monks speak of wisdom, but he had not understood what it was they were so excited about. Gradually he learned not only to open his heart with the memories of moments when his heart was full, he also learned that when his heart was full, he could call the wisdom from deep within his spirit to his conscious awareness. What a joy it was when he realized that wisdom was always there, responding to the need of each moment.

The old monk came again to Ming and told him it was time to put his new knowledge to the test. "Go out among the people. Listen, love, and let your spirit speak its wisdom. None of this power was given to us just for us. It is for everyone and we are simply instruments of compassion and wisdom. Test it. See if this is what fulfills your heart."

And so, Ming set out. He journeyed to villages, talked with people, spent time in silence and time in communication and friendship. He chose the connection with his heart again and again and again. He came to understand its quiet power and the impact of its wisdom.

And so his journey took him to the well that day, watching with compassion as the people of the village felt the fear of having to leave their homes and face the unknown.

CHAPTER 6
WISDOM AT THE WELL

Ming sat quietly on the stone bench by the well, holding the people of this village in the compassion of his heart. He was not worried or anxious as the men around him were. He was not wringing his hands as he saw the women doing in their conversations. He was at peace. In that moment, he rested in peace, holding those around him in compassion.

He focused on the women, recognizing that they held a deeper fear than the hunger, hardship, and privation that had gripped the men. He recognized their fear of the soldiers. Here they were far from the world that the soldiers controlled. This village was remote enough that armies did not come here. That meant that the soldiers did not grab their sons and husbands to fight in their wars or make the women their slaves. Here the women were safe from the soldiers; those they loved were protected.

Ming understood how valid their fear was. He remembered vividly the day the soldiers came upon him as he was caring for his flock of sheep in a mountain meadow.

When the soldiers appeared, the life Ming had known suddenly and irrevocably ended. Within moments he was

grabbed, bound, and gagged. The sheep he was watching over
scattered. However, sheep are not the smartest of creatures
and a number of them were quickly caught and slaughtered
as the soldiers prepared to take their food and their prisoner
back to their company.

Ming became a slave of the soldiers. As a young boy, he
was required to do the many tasks involved with feeding and
caring for an army on the move. The soldiers showed no pity
or understanding for the young boy as he struggled with the
overwhelming loss of his family. They shouted at him and
struck him to make him work harder.

Ming often worked with another young boy who also had
been captured. Late at night they would sometimes tell each
other of their families. They spoke of their fathers and their
mothers. For each one these were very special memories that
connected them to a life that seemed very far away. It was the
stories about the things they had done with their brothers and
sisters that at times brought a moment of laughter into their
difficult and exhausted lives.

As the weeks grew into months and then years, Ming grew
into a strong, resolute young man. The solders discovered
that in addition to his strength, he also had the quickness
and agility that make for a great warrior. They began to train
him as a fighter. As his skill increased, so did the respect he
received from the soldiers. Eventually, Ming was sent into his
first battle. Ming fought well and those who fought beside him
called him brave and fierce. With his success in battle, Ming's
life began to improve.

While the battle gave Ming new stature with the soldiers,
it also brought pain. His friend who had shared his memories
of home did not survive.

With these memories stirred by the women's fear, Ming felt
his compassion for the families deepen and expand. He knew,
perhaps better than they did, that the hardships they would
face would be difficult for all of them.

Ming also knew that worry and anxiety brought no solutions. He had learned that the answer was always there and would flow through the heart when it was ready or, more accurately, when he was ready to receive it. Turning his attention within himself, Ming made the monk's choice, the choice of his heart. From his heart he felt his spirit expanding his view.

He saw the men by the well. He saw the women in anxious conversation. He saw the children off playing because they had a special moment of not being attended to. He saw the houses and the hard earth that had been packed by many feet as it had become the streets between the houses. He saw the edge of the plateau beyond the town and the mountainsides rising above the town.

He saw the trees and rocks of the mountains. His eyes were drawn to a vibrant green patch on the mountainside. His heart spoke a simple thought into his brain. *That green means water.*

Ming smiled. His heart was full. This moment was one of his favorites, the moment his heart gave its wisdom. When his spirit gave its wisdom it often came as a simple statement to his mind; however, with that simple statement came a whole new realm of understanding.

The old monk had explained to Ming how spirit's wisdom came not as reason and deduction, rather as insight and understanding.

Ming enjoyed the understanding that now filled his awareness. He knew the villagers would not need to leave their homes. He also knew of the hard work ahead for them. He knew of the satisfaction that would, in a few days, fill their world and the celebration and happiness that would follow. He delighted in the experience of understanding. The understanding of the earth, the people, and the flow of possibilities that life offered in this moment.

Jain had drifted back to the monk. Perhaps as his friends became more upset and fearful it was the peace of the monk that attracted him, like a shelter in the storm of emotion that encircled him. It was also comforting to know that the monk understood the problem they were facing.

Jain said to the monk, "We need to gather our things to leave the village. Most of us will leave in the morning. Do you know in which direction there is enough water for our herds?"

The monk responded, "I am new to this area, and I came up through the main valley from the east. I will think on your question. I know it's important that your herds survive your journey."

Then Ming said to Jain, "I was noticing the vibrant green on that hillside up the mountain above us. It looks like you have good farmers here as well as herdsman."

"Yes, we do," Jain responded. "Their crops are plentiful, and our farmers have built terraces on the hillside to raise their crops."

"They must have a good water source to make the land so green," the monk replied.

"Oh, they do. There is a large spring and stream that flows into the valley that is over that ridge," Jain, said pointing to the hillside to their west. "That valley is a different drainage. It is very steep, and it is almost impassable. Even though there is water there, it is too steep to live there."

"How do the farmers get the water from the stream in the other drainage to their crops on this side?" the monk asked.

Jain explained how the farmers had learned to build ditches far up the mountainside that let them move the water down the mountain and over the ridge to the fields where they needed it.

Ming said to Jain, "You have many strong men in this village. Do you think you could build bigger ditches to bring more water from the other drainage? Is there enough over there to provide for the village?"

Jain stopped and silently looked up at the mountainside with Ming. His eyes widened, and suddenly he jumped up and ran to the men at the well.

"Listen, my friends. I know how we can get the water we need!" Jain exclaimed to the gathered villagers.

He explained his idea of building ditches like the farmers above them had. The ditches could move the water from the stream high above them over to their part of the mountain so it could flow through their town.

For a moment there was not a sound. Every man was scanning the hillside above him. Then, as through a dam had burst, they all started talking at once. Some men ran over to the women to tell them what they had figured out. They explained how they could build ditches to move the stream's water down the mountain into their valley and into their village. Soon there were a few moments of pandemonium as people ran about on their way to tell others and gather their tools. The square quickly emptied. The monk was left sitting quietly on the bench by the well. He had a serene smile on his face.

The monk joined the men in their work. He helped bring the jugs of water down the mountain as the families made do with carried water for the days it took to build the ditches. Ming worked with a joyful heart, enjoying the excitement of the men and their families. He was there the day they opened the ditches and the water flowed into the town, through the square where the well had been. There was more than enough water for the crops on the hillside, the flocks in the village, and the needs of the families.

Ming took special delight in the attention everyone paid to Jain, who had come up with the idea that saved their town. The monk got to know Shen and enjoyed his pride in his father. He remembered how good it had felt when he was young and had been proud of his father.

The monk was invited to many of the homes for meals and a place to sleep through those days. The villagers remembered that it was a blessing to have a monk in their houses, so Ming ate well and enjoyed the villagers, especially their children.

Then one morning, the monk was at the stream in the village when Jain and Shen brought their herd for their early morning drink. After greeting each other, the monk told them he would be traveling on, as his heart had told him it was time to leave.

Jain started saying good-bye, then stopped and looked at Ming as though seeing him for the first time. "That day, when the well went dry, you were the one who asked about the water on the hillside," Jain stated. "You asked about the ditches."

Ming smiled at this man who had become his friend. Ming responded, "You were the one who brought that insight to the others and who lifted their gaze from the empty well to the potential on the hillside." He added, "Good things happen when people open their hearts together."

Then with a wave to Shen, he turned and peacefully walked forth from the village in the direction his heart was calling him.

A beautiful stream now flows from the spring on the mountainside, down the ditches the villagers made and through the town where there is more than enough water for all.

Somewhere in the memory of that day, there was a monk who visited for a moment and helped them build the ditches. Then, with what they remember as great peace, he journeyed on his way.

PART 1B
TODAY

CHAPTER 7
THE MONK'S EXPERIENCE

I was a young boy when I first heard about Ming and the monk's choice. I imagined the monk as a sage, a wise person who walks from village to village.

When a sage enters a village, he joins the villagers. He experiences what is taking place in that village. If the villagers are fearful and angry, their anger might focus on the monk. That would be a natural response. After all, to the townspeople he would be a stranger. They would naturally think, "What is he doing here? Maybe he is the cause of our problems!"

When the anger focuses on the monk, he is able to make the monk's choice, the choice of the heart. As a result of that choice, he feels compassion and love for the people. He understands how hurt and afraid they must be to have such anger. As they express their anger at him, he lets it flow by like the wind of the storm and chooses to respond with compassion.

The storm may blow for a moment, but storms pass. The monk, who made the monk's choice, continues to experience within himself peace and compassion. He is there in the village when the storm of their anger has passed. Regardless of their choices, within himself the monk has made the choice to know peace and compassion because he has made the monk's choice

The monk will have experienced peace and compassion during his time in the village. His feelings will not change because of the behavior of others. However, because of his peace, because of his compassion, the world of the villagers will have changed. Because of the monk's choice, the village will have experienced both peace and wisdom.

As he travels from town to town, the monk finds that he has the wisdom to know when to speak and when to keep silent. He knows what to say and he knows how to listen. When the monk is in the presence of fear, he finds that he is guided to hope and wisdom. The monk is guided because he makes the monk's choice, the choice of his heart.

The monk is the presence in the story, and within us, of peace, compassion, and wisdom. He is guided to respond to what happens before him in ways that will fulfill his life and support those around him. These gifts are his because he has made the monk's choice, the choice of his heart.

There are two major shifts we can identify that happened within Ming. The first is the shift from the angry defensive reaction Ming felt in response to the villagers' anger at him. When anger is directed at the monk, his initial reaction is to attack those attacking him. This is not only a normal response; it was intensified because of Ming's years as a soldier. Ming finds his hand starting to reach for a weapon he was trained to use. Yet Ming is able to shift from this defensive reaction and make a different choice. He achieves instead a response of peace and compassion. As a result of that shift, he is able to respond with understanding to the villagers, thus diffusing the hostility.

The second major shift the monk experiences is the expansion of his awareness of a possible solution to replace the village's water. All of the villagers' attention was on the lack of water in the well and the threat to their well-being. But Ming's perception expands intuitively to recognize the presence of water evidenced by the green crops on the mountainside. With this shift of perception comes an understanding of how this water could be used to provide for the town's needs.

Each of these shifts, as well as subtler ones within the story, are the result of Ming's ability to make the monk's choice. Can we, you and I and others in similar situations, make the same kind of shifts Ming did? Is it possible today to learn how to make the monk's choice and move from defensiveness to peace or from limitation to solution?

Thanks to some breakthrough science that identifies how such shifts are made, we now know that it is possible. Because of people actively practicing these transformative techniques in their lives, we know that such shifts can be made in real-life situations. I have seen many people make these shifts over and over again as they experience daily challenges both large and small. This book is about how to make these shifts by making the monk's choice in our own lives.

CHAPTER 8

THE SCIENCE OF CHOICE

As a young man, I started searching to discover how I could make the transformative shifts that the monk experienced. In my search, I came across The HeartMath® Institute, where an amazing group of people was taking a scientific look at what causes human transformation.

Their scientists measured to see if there are specific changes in our bodies when we go from a lower level of performance to a higher one. They measured changes in the brain, the heart and other biological systems. They discovered that the first and most impactful of all the changes involved when such a transformation takes place, happens within the heart. Specific changes that they could measure in the heart caused the body and brain to transform, to go from a lesser level of performance to a greater one. Their findings revealed that the primary instrument of human transformation is the heart. To me, this was a profound discovery.

When the heart goes through a specific change, system after system of our personal biology is brought into its influence. The heart's changes result in changes to our brains and to our emotional responses. HeartMath's research revealed there is a very specific key, like an access code, that lifts people from a place of being stressed, blocked, frustrated, or unhappy into very real states of harmony, both physical and emotional. This was, in part, the same kind of transformative shift described in the monk's story.

Personally, I have found the measurable transformation in HeartMath's work very meaningful. Other techniques I tried resulted in changes that were subjective and difficult to measure. When comparing my experiences with someone else, it was difficult to know what had been achieved in our inner perceptions. With HeartMath's scientific approach, I could see the changes on their instruments. I was able to measure the difference between processes that were merely helpful and those that actually transformed biological systems from a lower level to a higher level of functioning.

I became so excited about these breakthroughs that I joined the HeartMath staff and spent more than seven years working with them, exploring and teaching these discoveries.

Their discoveries show us how to make a major transformation, not over years, but in minutes. I will share some of this breakthrough science with you as we examine how to make this transformative choice, the monk's choice.

How do we choose our hearts as the monk did in the story? How do we experience peace and wisdom instead of anger and confusion?

I have found that today — not all the time, but often — people are able to make the monk's choice, the choice of their hearts. That choice makes it possible to experience compassion in response to fear, peace in response to lack, and love in response to hate. These are to me the same choices the monk was making in this ancient tale.

There is another result from the monk's choice that is as valuable to me as the experience of compassion or the experience of peace. Perhaps it is the most valuable gift of all: the gift of wisdom.

Each time I seek to make the monk's choice, I am given the additional gift of access to a deeper level of understanding and insight than I had been experiencing. In making the monk's choice we access our deeper wisdom.

In each situation where I apply the monk's choice, I find I understood the situation from the place of a greater wisdom. A shift of perception takes place within me and I understand how to address the challenge before me in a way that was not clearly present before making the monk's choice.

The HeartMath research validates this experience of a greater wisdom within us. Researchers there call it "heart intelligence" and identify it as the master intelligence of the human system. That's important. The wisdom accessed through our hearts is not just one of the many intelligences within the human system. It is the "master intelligence." Wow!

The scientists were able to measure the physical changes that open our access to this higher level of intelligence. They described the heart's intelligence as a separate domain of intelligence from that of the brain. It operates differently and its contributions are distinct from the intelligence of our brains. They were also able to compare its effectiveness to the brain's intelligence, finding it different and, in many cases, more effective than that of our brains.

In addition to feeling truly liberated by the wisdom available to me through my heart, I treasure the peace I find in these experiences. I treasure the discovery that the monk's peace can be mine.

When I make the monk's choice, I'm not stressed anymore. I'm not worried anymore. I am at peace. I feel both the peace of no conflict and the peace of serenity. I experience a deep, peaceful feeling I can best describe as fulfillment. When we are worried, challenged, angry, anxious, or frustrated, we do not feel fulfilled. When I make the monk's choice, part of the feeling of fulfillment is a beautiful feeling of peace.

Ming had access to something that brought a greater understanding of the challenges before him. The monk understood the villagers' experience. In addition, he was connected to a level of wisdom that held a solution to the challenges – both the challenges facing the villagers and the challenges facing the monk.

What gave him peace? What gave him the strength not to be overwhelmed by the actions of others? What is it that lifts you and me above the emotional fracas around us, yet keeps us connected with the people involved? What is it that connects us to a greater level of wisdom capable of guiding us in the challenges of our lives?

I'm sure there are many names for that greater something. I know many different cultures, spiritual paths, and religious traditions have given this a name, as has the psychological and sociological studies of our time.

I've looked at many of these names and descriptions. The conclusion I have come to is that, for me, it doesn't matter what we call it or how we define it. To me, it matters only if we connect with it.

As we explore the transformative connection to our greater wisdom, I will occasionally refer to the place we find this wisdom as our spiritual heart. This is my understanding from my years of working with our spiritual natures. I perceive the spiritual heart as the innate wisdom we each possess in the spiritual part of ourselves, as opposed to our mental or emotional selves. HeartMath simply calls it "heart intelligence."

What is important is not its name. What is important is that we learn how to access that deeper level of wisdom to meet the challenges in our villages.

Just as Ming entered a village with its particular problem, we also enter and interact in different groups or situations that are our "villages." Our workplace, friendships, social connections, spiritual or religious organizations, public organizations, national and international allegiances, families and, equally important, our view of ourselves are all "villages" we enter and engage with.

One of the most impactful villages we enter into most often is our families. Because we care so deeply about what these people closest to us think and feel, we can easily be triggered by what happens in that village.

The following experience was especially inspiring to me, for many reasons. The monk in this village recognized his reaction to what was taking place in his family and consciously made the monk's choice.

CHAPTER 9
PETER'S CHOICE

The monk in this story is my son, Peter. Peter has a wonderful wife whose name is Julia. They live in Los Angeles. They have the natural challenges of young people in making enough money to pursue their dreams, to find the opportunities that empower their lives, and to make the decisions that let their lives go forward wisely and abundantly.

Peter shared with me that Julia received a job offer that would be a very demanding position for her. She had been doing temporary work at a company that recognized her skills and wanted to bring her aboard in a permanent position. The offer to Julia was inviting financially; however, it was very challenging in terms of what would be asked of her. She was aware of problems and dysfunction that had resulted in the position being vacant. As she looked at the positive and negative aspects of this job possibility, she became very upset, anxious, and worried. She began to experience an anxiety attack. Anxiety attacks had challenged her earlier in her life.

Peter wanted so much to help his wife. He saw her tension, anxiety, and worry. When I was on the HeartMath staff, Peter found that he appreciated the effectiveness of their techniques and had taken some of their courses so he could teach these skills to others. As a result, Peter had been trained in how to transform stress in a moment. He knew the techniques the monk knew. Peter realized he could use those skills to quickly help Julia overcome her anxiety and get to a wise decision.

Peter knew these skills would literally change the patterns of Julia's heart so that she would no longer feel overwhelmed and anxious. Without this emotional angst, she would be able to access her deeper wisdom to guide her on whether or not to accept the job offer.

Peter's desire to lead his wife through this powerful technique was tempered by the fact that he had tried it before. Julia was receptive and had worked with these techniques on her own. However, Peter had also seen that when she was really upset, she resented his bringing up this way of working. He understood from their past experience that this may not be a teaching moment for her.

As Peter watched and listened to Julia express her stress, he began to feel frustrated and powerless. Powerlessness was a natural reaction for Peter; in loving his wife, feeling her pain, having a way to help her and yet knowing he could not give her relief because his role in this situation was as her husband, not as her stress coach. Aware of his frustration, he realized that the answer was not about using the technique for Julia. He realized the help he needed in that moment was to use this skill for himself.

Peter did this using a simple set of steps called the Heart Wisdom Tool that is based on HeartMath's research. Using this simple technique, he was able to make the monk's choice. He connected with his heart and activated the access code that connected him to his wisdom.

Within a minute or two. Peter made that connection with his deeper wisdom. His stress, frustration, and worry about Julia were gone. In their place he felt his compassion and love for her. Peter asked his wisdom what response he could make to Julia that would help her in this situation. The answer he got surprised him. It was not about sharing the wonderful knowledge that he had on how to transform anxiety and get answers. It was about what his wife needed, right in that moment.

His wisdom told him to ask her if she would like to be held. So he asked. Julia stopped for a moment and then responded that yes, she did want to be held. She let Peter hold her and they connected. The tension began to abate, and the love Peter felt for her began to seep through the anxiety and tension she carried. A little while later, she felt better. It was then that Julia turned to him and thanked him for knowing what to do to help her and specifically for "not saying anything." Because Peter had taken the steps to connect with his wisdom before responding, he knew to do just that. He couldn't help but smile a little.

Julia was able to move beyond her emotional turmoil and access her deeper wisdom. She recognized she had the ability to deal with the dysfunctions she had recognized in the position offered to her, so she took the job and has been successful at it. The greater income let her provide for her family, as was her heart's desire.

In the village we call family, we interact with people we love, know well, and whose challenges we feel deeply about and are impacted by. This is a wonderful place to respond with the compassion and wisdom of the monk.

CHAPTER 10
THE SECRET

What is the secret the monk knew? What is the secret Peter used when he felt so concerned over Julia's anxiety?

This secret gets us to an amazing source of wisdom within us. It shifts how we perceive our world. It changes what we feel and how we respond to life.

I'm calling this a "secret" because it seems to elude us in our daily living. I have worked with many teachers who share self-help and personal growth skills. Yet, most are not aware of this secret that causes such powerful personal transformation.

This secret is not the use of the analysis skills we learned in our educational institutions. Rather than using our brains to try to think about something in a different way, this secret connects us to the power of our spiritual selves flowing through our hearts. That power creates a major shift in how we view, feel about, and respond to the situation before us.

The secret actually creates a shift in our perception. Once we activate this secret capacity, we look at a situation in a new way, which means we understand it differently from the way our minds did a moment before. Peter's realization that Julia needed to be held was very different from how he viewed her need and his role before activating the secret.

Scientific researchers discovered this secret when they were exploring the presence of the greater intelligence that had been identified within our hearts. They were following the clues that began with research in the 1960's, when scientists first realized that the heart sends a signal to the brain and the brain makes a different choice based on directions from the heart. That sure surprised the scientists!

Researchers at the HeartMath Institute built on those discoveries as they continued to explore this intelligence of the heart. They discovered that when the heart makes a very specific, measurable change, we are able to access a deeper level of wisdom within ourselves. They describe this wisdom as a "distinct domain" of intelligence. I label this domain of intelligence with the term that describes what we experience when it is activated. What we experience is wisdom. The HeartMath researchers call it "heart intelligence." This wisdom becomes available to us through our hearts.

The physical changes that make this wisdom available can be clearly measured scientifically. Its impact on the brain and on what we feel is astounding.

The researchers found that these changes in the heart cause our emotional process to change because they impact the part of our brain that directs our emotional functioning. They also found that the processing capacity of the cognitive function of the brain increases as the heart patterns interact with the systems we use to think.

Their tests reveal that a more effective level of decision-making is activated by these changes in the heart. There is a measurable level of improvement in the physical, mental, emotional, and decision-making elements of our systems. These improvements are not incremental. Rather than just improving these systems a little bit, they evidence a significantly higher or more effective state of functioning.

The secret that the scientists discovered was that these transformative changes in the heart are activated when we experience a very specific set of positive feelings. The specific set of feelings that activate the transformative patterns of the heart are the deeply held feelings of the heart. These feeling include appreciation, care, compassion, peace, and love.

We will look at this category of feelings, what it includes and what it does not include, later on in the book. Let's begin exploring this powerful secret by focusing on one of the heart feelings that the monk, Ming, used.

Compassion is one of the choices the monk made. Ming responded to the people around him by feeling compassion for them in their difficult situation. Ages later. the HeartMath scientists would discover that the feeling of compassion is one of the triggers that initiates this transformative cascade of changes within the body. Compassion activates our connection with our hearts.

Compassion is also a feeling we can access once the heart has done its transformative work on the body. Even if we can't feel our compassion as the challenge before us develops, after we access the heart we are able to feel compassion for those around us. This is important, because compassion is a direct connector to our deepest wisdom. It is also important because, as in the monk's story, most of our challenges involve people.

Compassion expands our understanding of people and their actions. It connects us with wisdom. The heart changes give us access to a clear, measurable experience of a greater level of wisdom.

When I first heard the monk's story, something in me grabbed hold of the idea that we have the capacity within us not to give away the power to choose what we feel. I believed that there was a way to stay in the beautiful feeling of peace that the monk's story inspired in me. I knew intuitively that it was possible to choose compassion. I sought ways to discover how to make that choice. My search has been a diligent and meaningful one, spanning many years.

As the years passed, I had very powerful experiences that showed me this inner peaceful response was possible. I know we can respond with compassion to the anger and projections of others. I don't doubt that you have also had those insights. I'm sure there have been moments when you personally made that choice. Like the monk, you have chosen your heart and felt compassion for others in their difficulties.

My challenge was that I did not know how to do it at will. I could only make the choice on rare occasions. It was not my natural reaction.

When people liked me, it was easy for me to feel love and appreciation for them. If they shared a problem with me, I easily felt compassion. However, when they were angry or critical, or if they felt pain and expressed that by striking out at me, I ended up responding to them from fear and defensiveness and not with the compassion I would have liked to use.

Our brains are wired to respond to stimuli by checking it against our emotional memory. If our brains find any negative emotional association (like pain, fear, or emotional hurt) with the stimuli (someone's words, attitude, or behavior), even if it is not direct, those emotions or stimuli can trigger our fight-flight reaction, what the medical people call our stress response. We respond with defensiveness, attack, or withdrawal. It is hard-wired in us.

Eventually I discovered that after a momentary reaction, we do have another option. After our initial reactive impulse, the monk's choice becomes available to us. I did not have to try to never feel anger, defensiveness, or resentment. My challenge was to make the monk's choice in the moments after I felt those things.

I explored many paths and disciplines that spoke of peace and compassion. In those explorations, I found a lot of supportive and encouraging ideas and teachings. However, I did not find a consistently effective technique that could transform the energy in my feelings of defensiveness until I became involved with the HeartMath research.

The change within the heart — this change that opens the physical heart and lets a greater level of love and wisdom flow through it from our spiritual heart — is activated by a feeling.

More accurately, it is activated by heart feelings. Compassion is one of those feelings.

Not any feeling will activate this change. Anger, hurt, frustration, and jealousy are very natural feelings we all have. However, they do not come from, nor do they open, our hearts. Only those personal feelings that are positive, uplifting, and rooted in our core values have the power to bring about the transformation of our hearts.

Compassion is one of the powerful experiences the monk's story spoke of. It is what Peter felt for Julia as she was trapped in her anxiety. Compassion is one of the access codes to the deepest wisdom of our spiritual hearts.

CHAPTER 11
THE HEART WISDOM TOOL*

Now let's look at the question of how. How do we access our hearts? We know the secret that positive, uplifting feelings of our hearts, such as compassion, bring about this transformation. How do we get to those feelings when the person in front of us is not inspiring one of these feelings? How do we put this secret to work for us? How do we choose our hearts? How do we enter the portal that connects us to our spiritual selves?

I call my favorite technique the Heart Wisdom Tool.

The Heart Wisdom Tool is very simple; if you focus on the steps and intentionally take each step, it will work for you. Let me explain this technique that helped Peter and has helped thousands of people end their stress and access their deepest wisdom.

The Heart Wisdom Tool consists of three steps:
> Step 1: Touch and Breathe
> Step 2: Remember and Feel
> Step 3: Sincerely Ask

---

* The Heart Wisdom Tool is an adaption of the HeartMath® technique Freeze-Frame® published with permission granted to David McArthur by Quantum Intech, Inc.

Step 1: Touch and Breathe

Step 1 begins when you touch your heart. When you bring your hand to your chest and touch your heart area you begin a shift of energy from your head to your heart. Touch your heart now. As you do so pretend to breathe through your heart. Pretend to take several long, deep breaths through your heart. As you do this, you are removing your attention from the head's focus and directing your attention on the area around your heart.

Step 2: Remember and Feel

Do you remember when we were talking about our heart feelings? One of the things I discovered by using this technique is that when I experience those feelings my heart feels full.

Feeling love makes your heart feel full. Remember a time when your heart felt full. Remember that delicious feeling. Maybe it is a moment when you got a hug from a grandchild or someone you loved very deeply. Remember that wonderful feeling. Maybe it was a special day – a wedding or a graduation. Perhaps it was an amazing moment in nature with dolphins jumping around you, or maybe it was just coming home and your dog was excited and waving his tail so enthusiastically you could feel his love and delight.

Remember one of those moments when your heart was full. Feel that wonderful feeling again. Don't get involved in thinking about it, just remember the feeling and let yourself feel the feeling. This powerful feeling is an expression of love caught in the experience of that moment. It is an experience of some aspect of love. The feelings that are a part of love are the access code to your heart.

As you spend a little time feeling that feeling, you may sense your body shift. You will feel better as any anxiety or other negative feelings release. Enjoy that feeling of remembering your love in the form it took in that beautiful memory. Enjoy that full heart feeling as you experience it today.

Step 3: Sincerely Ask

The third step is to Sincerely Ask. This is the point when you draw the wisdom from your spiritual heart to your conscious awareness. Ask your heart, "What is a more effective response to this situation?" It is a simple but powerful question.

When Peter did this, he got the instruction to offer to hold Julia. He received a clear response that not only instructed him what to do, but also gave him an understanding of how to do it. He understood how to make it her choice so that in a moment when she felt powerless, she could feel her power to choose. The power to draw the wisdom of your spiritual heart into your conscious awareness is the power of your sincerity. Sincerely ask, and your spiritual heart will respond. The key to the effectiveness of this step is the sincerity of your asking.

In the monk's story, Ming used the question, "What is my heart's direction for this situation?" Like Peter, he was opening to receive the wisdom of his spiritual heart so he could respond effectively to the situation before him.

Step 1: Touch and Breathe
Step 2: Remember and Feel
Step 3: Sincerely Ask

These three steps can help you access your heart feelings, transform your system, and give you answers to the challenges before you. They are the practical tools that heighten your resiliency. You end up not being exhausted by your challenges; rather, you end up empowered.

If you would like more information on this powerful technique, I invite you to explore it more extensively in my book, *Your Spiritual Heart*. With the steps I have shared above, you have the essential elements to make the same choice the monk made. You can now access your deepest wisdom, just as the monk did.

9

CHAPTER 12
HEART FEELINGS

I have had the good fortune to know people who have success-fully responded to challenging situations in the "villages" in their lives. Some experienced an impact on those around them that was similar to the impact attributed to our monk in the story. Like Peter, they were able to remember to choose their hearts.

As you discovered with the Heart Wisdom Tool, the steps to making the monk's choice, the choice of your heart, are not difficult. I often find that the most difficult part of the process is remembering to make the choice in the midst of a challenging situation.

I believe there is a quality in the lives of those who remem-ber to make this choice that makes it easier to achieve. People who have made the commitment to choose their hearts in the challenges before them often work at developing "a relationship with their hearts." As a result, when challenging situations arose, they already have a good, strong relationship with their hearts. They believe that relationship makes it easier to remember to choose their hearts.

I invested many years of schooling – classrooms, tests, home-work, study sessions, etcetera – through which I developed my relationship with my brain. As a result, when challenges came along, my brain naturally activated and began to give me answers from its level of intelligence. There were certainly many situations when my brain provided a helpful, effective response to the questions before me. As a society we have valued and encouraged each other to develop a good working relationship with our brains. But that is different from developing a relationship with our hearts.

In the monk's tale, it seems fair to assume that developing a relationship with his heart would be natural for a monk. We generally think of a monk as a person who has made a commitment to a path of peace and love. That commitment suggests that in one's daily life, the individual dedicates time to focus on love and related feelings such as peace.

In general, monks seek to practice peace. Living monastically is to many people a symbol of a personal commitment to seek peace in the very small things that can be upsetting as well as in the larger ones. This is true whether we place our tale in the Orient, the Middle East, France, Africa, Argentina, New York City, or an indigenous culture. In the monastic traditions around the world, one of the universal practices is to spend time in some experience of one's heart.

One of the prime ways we increase our relationship with our hearts, and thus our effectiveness at making the monk's choice, begins with getting to know our heart feelings. In the coming chapters, we will explore the tremendous power that is unleashed by your heart feelings — feelings such as compassion, peace, joy, fulfillment, serenity, care, and appreciation.

The access code to our heart is found in our heart feelings. Specifically, heart feelings are those that are a part of the broader feeling we call love. Love is its most powerful and most direct access code to our spiritual hearts. Love transforms our mental, emotional, and physical systems. Yet love is experienced a little differently by every person.

When the HeartMath scientists began their research, they realized that love was a very broad, complex feeling with many elements that might be experienced differently by different people. To test their hypotheses, they needed to use a more specific feeling than love.

So they began with the feeling of appreciation. Appreciation is a very specific feeling. If you appreciate someone and I appreciate someone, our feelings will be fairly similar. The scientists discovered that the feeling of appreciation triggers this change in the heart that results in transformation of many bodily systems.

They found the same response is created by feelings of care and compassion. The response was also there for feelings of deep joy and serenity.

Heart Feelings

These are core heart feelings. Each of these transformative feelings is a part of love. If you love someone, you appreciate that person. If you love someone and that person is hurting, you feel compassion. These core heart feelings are the feelings that result in our hearts feeling the sense of fullness we have identified as present with the transformative heart feelings. All of them are a part of love.

Right now, if you feel the joy of remembering a special moment and let that feeling really soak in, you will discover that your anxiety will fade and positive feelings will appear. You are suddenly not stressed. You begin to see the questions before you from a different perspective. These changes are all measurable. Knowing how to access them through techniques such as the Heart Wisdom Tool has supported many people in living their lives at a higher, more fulfilling level.

Once you remember your "heart-filled moment" and enter into its heart feeling, the biophysical transformation takes place. At that point, the greater wisdom of your spiritual heart moves you into the most effective heart feeling response to the situation. For the monk, that effective heart feeling was compassion; for Peter, it was both compassion and his love for Julia. Your deep heart feelings have now opened the doorway to your deeper wisdom that will guide you in dealing with the situation successfully.

There is a place within us all where our spiritual nature is freed to express its greater wisdom and power. It uplifts us and gives us the direction to meet what life puts before us. That place within you is your spiritual heart. You can enter it easily by using the access code of the many rich, beautiful, uplifting feelings of your heart. The more often you go there, the greater your relationship with your heart.

I appreciated the following simple story of a monk named Meilin. Her heart feeling of compassion for the people of the village she enters was great because she knew from her life before becoming a monk the pain and struggle of hunger.

PART II
LIVING

PART 2A

LONG AGO

~ MEILIN ~

CHAPTER 13
A HUNGRY BOY

The young boy struggled to keep the bundle of wood on his back. He felt his legs shaking as he put one foot in front of the other trying to go up the hill. The wood felt so heavy. The boy had almost half the hill to climb before he could give the wood to the man who had promised him money. He tried to focus on the money that he could use to buy food. He was so hungry. It had been a long time since he had anything to eat. He had to get the wood to the man's house. As he took another step, his body seemed to run out of energy and he found himself sinking to his knees on the hard-packed earth of the road.

Then the burden of the wood seemed to lift. It was suddenly lighter. It almost lifted him up. He found his feet again and stood up, but the wood still felt light on his back. He looked up and saw the smiling face of a monk. Was it a monk? It was a woman, but she had on the long gray robe of a monk and she was lifting his bundle of wood.

"It would be best if you rested a moment before you continue on with this heavy bundle," she said as she smiled at him. "I was sitting on a bench in the shade under that tree. Please join me." As she spoke, she lifted his wood to her back and walked to the stone bench.

As the boy approached her bench the monk, whose name was Meilin, had a chance to look at him carefully. His threadbare clothing and emaciated body told its own story of hunger and deprivation. She reached into the bag she carried over her shoulder and brought out the wrapped gift of food that had been given to her that morning by a woman who had asked her to take it for herself or someone she might meet upon the road who had need of food.

"Before you pick up your wood again, you might eat this to give you some energy." She held the folded leaves containing the desperately needed food out to the boy. In an instant his thin hands snatched the food from hers. It was gone in a moment, inhaled by the boy. She could see the desperation on his face and the surprise as well.

She almost laughed at the surprised look on his face. However, she understood only too well the pain and desperation of hunger. "Do not be surprised that people share food with you. People are very generous. It gives them pleasure to help another. It is a blessing to them to give. This food was given to me to share with someone who might be in need.

"Now tell me how a young boy such as yourself finds himself in this town with such a big load of wood and so little to eat."

There on the stone bench under the shade of an ancient tree, with the load of wood at his feet, the young boy, whom the monk learned was called Xiang, told of being sent away to this town by his father, who explained there was no food in their village. His father believed he was old enough to survive and would be able to find food.

As he told his tale with the pure honesty only the young have, the monk felt the tug upon her heart. She felt her compassion for the people of the boy's village. She understood the desperation of this family and the pall of hunger that enfolded this child.

She was aware of the abundance that was expressed in the bustling town around her. Yet here was a child who had known little but hunger. She knew as a seeker of wisdom for many years that there were answers for life's challenges. As the boy described the hunger of his mother, father, and sisters, Meilin felt her heart reach out to the struggling family even though they were far away. She did not know the answers to the problems of the distant village the boy had left. However, she did know there was a source for those answers because she had sought that source often. Over the years she had come to value that seeking. Meilin became aware through the feeling of compassion in her heart that she felt a desire to make the journey to this village the young boy was describing to her.

She encouraged Xiang to complete his delivery and accept the money so he could buy the food he needed. Then she told him how to find a house she knew of where people cared for children and always had a meal for those who came to their door.

Xiang returned to his wood and pulling it upon his back, he continued his uphill journey. The monk watched him go and then, knowing her next steps could take her in a new direction, she made a choice, the monk's choice. That choice was not an outer direction; rather, it was an inner one. With the monk's choice, Meilin was taking steps to open herself to glimpse the choices that were before her. She was seeking to see clearly which path held the most meaning for the work of her soul.

Meilin was aware of the feelings of compassion her knowledge of the boy's hungry village called forth from her heart. As a monk who traveled throughout the countryside, Meilin often saw suffering and knew that one of the most powerful forces she could bring to those experiences was her compassion. She also clearly understood that in some of those situations, engaging with the people or their struggles was not hers to do.

In some situations, she would simply extend the compassionate feelings from her heart to those involved. Then she would give a blessing for healing and continue on her way. She knew she was not the healer of all things, yet she also knew she could be a beneficial presence. Often, her wisdom showed her that in some situations, a moment of her compassion was enough. That was all that was hers to do, and she was to continue on her way.

However, there had been other experiences where her heart had guided her to engage more fully with the people whose difficulty she had come across. The wisdom of her heart guided her to enter and share the burden the people shared. At those times, she knew that her love and compassion made it easier for the people to meet their challenges. Her presence and her wisdom became a part of a flow of power that helped people move through and transform a difficult situation. When her heart guided her to say "yes" to engage in those situations more fully, she found meaning and fulfillment in the events that followed, even when they were difficult for herself and the others involved.

Only days before, she had listened while a bitter rivalry between town leaders had begun to escalate to violence, a violence that frightened their families. Fortunately, Meilin's heart understood the power of forgiveness and the small steps that could open that larger door. She felt grateful as she remembered families responding and eventually returning to feeling safe again, with children free to play and their mothers returning to friendships that were a part of that village's strength.

This is why Meilin took a moment to make the monk's choice. This is why she asked and listened to the clarifying wisdom that flowed from her heart. It only took a moment, a beautiful moment, a moment of peace and clarity. After that moment, she rose and, slinging her bag over her shoulder, she set her path in a new direction. Her feet took her toward the distant mountains, toward the boy's village of hunger.

CHAPTER 14
VILLAGE OF HUNGER

As Meilin left the bustling town behind and began her journey past green fields filled with growing crops, she found herself reflecting on the experience the boy's struggle had awakened in her. She remembered the dull ache of hunger she had known as a young girl and the desperation it had brought to her own parents' eyes. She remembered with relief the crops finally being harvested and sitting down to a full bowl of rice. She did not know what it was that was trapping the boy's village in hunger, but her compassion embraced the people and her feet went forward step-by-step to be there with them.

The village the boy had described was several days' journey away. Meilin loved walking through the countryside. As a monk her presence was regarded as a blessing by the people she passed. She knew she would see many different people on the road. She watched and extended her blessing to the merchants and their carts, people walking to visit family, soldiers — some mounted, some on foot — on their errands. She sent thoughts of appreciation to the local people who tended the fields on either side of the road. Meilin knew there existed a strong belief that to harm a monk was to bring a life-long curse upon you, so she traveled without trepidation.

Late afternoon on her third day of walking, after climbing a steep pass, she crested a ridge and entered a much dryer land. It was a part of the great mountains to which she had not journeyed before. The road led her into an arid valley where the fields were few and their produce appeared meager. As she descended the trail she could tell from the dryness of the grasses, which were more yellow than green, that the rains had been few that year. She understood that the crops would not have been plentiful.

It was mid-morning of her fourth day of travel when Meilin entered the village the boy had described. It was small, perhaps only a dozen houses. In an open area by the well she saw a small market of several cloths spread on the ground on which clothing or simple items for trade were displayed. It told her she had arrived on market day. There was very little being offered in this market, however.

As the monk made her way to the shade of a large tree by the well, she was acutely aware of the emaciated, haunted look of the people. They walked with the shuffling gait of people who had no energy. Even though some had clothes that were colorful and bright, their bodies seemed depleted, as did their spirits. Meilin felt her heart open with compassion as she watched them pass by.

She saw the suspicion on their faces. It was natural for people to see a stranger as a threat when they did not have enough food for themselves. She knew that under different circumstances many of these people would have welcomed her and shared freely from their tables. It was a painful part of hunger that the natural generosity of their hearts was diminished by the fear of not enough.

Eventually a little girl broke away from the group of women gathered by the well and approached where the monk was sitting. She asked if Meilin would like some water. Meilin had watched as the little girl spotted her and run to ask her mother. When the mother saw her gray robe and recognized her as a monk, the mother at first had hesitated. Then she told her daughter it was all right to talk to the monk, but only to offer her water. The first contact with the children was a favorite moment for Meilin. She enjoyed watching their inquisitive eyes as their curiosity overcame the natural fear of the unknown to connect with a stranger.

Because it was well known to be a blessing to give to a monk, the gift of water at the well was almost always the first way village people connected with this new person in their midst. Usually after the water was shared, she would be given some food or invited to a meal in a family's home. The monk knew that those offers of food would be scarce in this village. When people were experiencing hunger, sharing was very difficult to do. She had not come here to be well-fed or cared for. She had come here to join with the people in their experience. Hunger.

Meilin went with the little girl who introduced herself as Chen. She met Chen's mother, Nuo, and began to learn the story of the series of crop failures from years of little rain that had brought the scourge of hunger to this village.

The monk asked if Nuo knew the family of the little boy, Xiang, she had met carrying the wood in the town, now many days away. The mother sent Chen to call Xiang's mother to hear from the monk who had seen her son. Nuo then opened up easily to Meilin, finding her understanding and compassion a huge relief after years of facing the growing struggle to feed and care for her family.

Suddenly they spotted a woman running toward them. It was Xiang's mother, who broke down in tears when she heard that her son was safe. Meilin told of the family who fed children that she had sent the boy to and about his effort to earn food by delivering wood for money.

It was not long before the story of the monk's connection with Xiang spread through the village, and more people gathered to ask if Meilin had heard of their relatives and to hear the news of the world outside their village. The monk was gratified as she saw suspicion fade from people's faces as her connection with the outside communities brought a glimmer of life and connection beyond this harsh corner of the world.

Nuo was too embarrassed to invite the monk to her home because she dared not offer her any of the thin soup they would share as their evening meal. She did tell her of a place where she could sleep where she would not feel the cold of the night so acutely.

As the shadows began to lengthen and the villagers retired to their homes, Meilin touched her heart and began the slow breathing she often used to calm her body. She knew she was not her body. Her body could be hungry, yet she was not. She chose to be at peace in that moment and to feed her soul with the spiritual food she experienced as the feelings of love. The love feeling nourished her spirit even as her body wished for physical food. She knew how to do this because over her years as a monk, Meilin had built a strong relationship with her heart. By choosing to activate her feelings of love, Meilin was making what she knew to be the monk's choice, the choice of her heart.

She breathed in the feeling of beauty and joy she had experienced as she remembered the morning's first bird song. Her heart filled with appreciation of the exquisite sound of each note that had come forth from the tiny, feathered creature. She felt uplifting energy filling her heart as she remembered the laughter of children at play she had seen that day. She felt a deep inner joy as she remembered watching the shy yet curious eyes of the little girl who had offered her the gift of water. With each breath she drew the beauty and the uplifting energy deeper into herself as the feeling of love flowing in and through every cell of her being. It filled her. It lifted her. It filled all her senses and overflowed as powerful waves of love flowing from her heart. She rested in the magnificence of that love. For a while she sent these exquisite feelings out into the community around her. She rested in its peace. Sometime later, as her attention returned to the world around her, she sat quietly, seeing in her mind each person she had met that day with the eyes of her heart. She could see in each one the

VILLAGE OF HUNGER   81

beauty, the magnificence that had been revealed to her vision by her awakened heart.

The next day, the monk was again sitting by the well. Early in the morning she had walked through the town with her prayers of blessing for the people. The people smiled at her presence but there had been no offer of food, nor did she expect any. Meilin again made the monk's choice and spent time in the inner experience, remembering the feelings of love that fed her soul and strengthened her as her body struggled with the pain of hunger.

The little girl, Chen, came running up to her that day when she saw Meilin sitting under the tree by the well. Even though Chen was thin and frail, the excitement of a new friend brought a smile to her face. More of the village people who came to the village well that morning took a moment to acknowledge her. The monk knew the news she had brought would quickly spread around the small village. Perhaps the people felt more comfortable with her because she was a little less of a stranger this day. Perhaps it was also because she did not eat nor ask for food.

Chen now talked to her and told her she was hungry. The monk noticed the little girl was trying not to let her mother know what she was saying. Meilin told her that she, too, felt hunger in her body, yet she was not her body and so she chose to fast from food and fill herself with love instead, which helped to free her from the call of food, even if just for a moment.

Meilin told Chen she had learned how to remember she was not her body by using a secret that the monk knew. She asked Chen if she would like to learn this secret. The child eagerly responded. Meilin told her the secret was called "the monk's choice." It was a way to move from the mind that was run by her body to the mind that was run by her spirit. "Would you like to do it with me?" Meilin asked. With Chen's eager response, the monk had her touch her heart and pretend that she could breathe through her heart. As Chen did this, Meilin told her she was now at the doorway to the part of her that was more than her body.

Next, Meilin told her to remember a moment when her heart was so full it felt like dancing. Chen quickly responded that her heart danced when her puppy would try to lick her face when she first arrived at home. The puppy would jump up and down and hop all around because it was so glad to see her. Meilin told her to remember how wonderful that felt and to hold that wonderful feeling in her heart. As Chen did this, the monk watched the child's smile grow bigger and bigger. "That is wonderful," Meilin replied. "Let that special feeling keep filling you up so you can feel it everywhere in your body." As the child did this, Meilin asked her, "Do you feel hungry now, Chen?" Chen said, "No, I feel wonderful!"

Meilin explained to Chen that she felt so good because she was in her spirit self. In her spirit self, the hunger that is there is fulfilled by the love she was experiencing through remembering her feelings for the puppy. The monk had Chen send some of that wonderful feeling to her body, to the part of her that felt so hungry. She could see that Chen was very focused as she followed the instruction. "Now," said Meilin, "give your body a big hug." After Chen hugged herself, she opened her eyes and saw Meilin's smile. "You can do that whenever the feeling of hunger gets too strong," Meilin told her. "The power of the love does not take the hunger away. Your body is still hungry. The love makes the hunger less powerful and the part of you that is not hungry is much stronger. Remember when things are hard, that is a good time for you to make the monk's choice."

Meilin asked Chen if she would like to hear another secret. Chen again responded with a child's beautiful receptivity. The monk explained to her that another way to help when you did not have enough was to give something away. She suggested that Chen find something she liked and give it to a friend. Chen became excited at giving something away and said she had a special white stone she could give to her friend. The monk told her that was an excellent idea, encouraging her to be sure and do it that day.

Chen's mother Nuo came over and spoke with the monk. As they talked, Meilin asked her about the beautiful red color of the dress that Chen and her mother wore. Nuo told her the color came from dying their cloth with the resin of a bush that grew in the crags above the valley, which created this beautiful red color that the villagers loved. Because their existence was so harsh, the villagers used the color to add vibrancy and pleasure to their lives. She said that to them it was the color of hope.

"I don't know how we can have hope anymore. We don't have enough food and it has been so for a long time. The crops, even when we are able to harvest, do not appear to be enough to care for all our needs. I am always hungry, as are Chen and my husband. We have a few goats he cares for and to eat them would stop our milk supply, which we need to survive. We don't have the money to get any more goats and our small field produces very little because of the lack of rain. It is hopeless."

"I understand hopelessness," Meilin said. "I remember a year of starvation where I almost died. Many people in our village did die."

CHAPTER 15
HUNGRY CHILD TO MONK

Although many years had passed, Meilin could still vividly remember the feeling of constant hunger. She remembered when her mother would return from a day spent in the fields trying to glean grain and dig up roots while watching the goats of a neighbor, for which she received a small cup of goat milk. They would soak the few grains and sometimes cook the roots in a pot or in the coals. It was so little to eat. They would sleep fitfully, without rest, as their bodies demanded food to end the pain and ache that had become a constant presence in their lives.

Meilin's father had been taken away to war and Meilin's mother did what she could, but it was not much. Sometimes a neighbor would share a small bit of food, an amount that seemed to the two of them like a feast. Meilin had swept the doorways of homes where perhaps the people would give her money or a bite of food. However, this was a time when there were so many people hungry that the doors would mostly remain shut and Meilin would go away hungry.

And then the day came when Meilin's mother could not get up to go out to the fields. Meilin stayed by her mother's side but there was little she could do. It was only a few days until her mother stopped breathing. The neighbors helped take her mother's body to be buried, but they could do little else.

Meilin was alone. Her mother had been her strength. Even when they had nothing, her mother would wrap her in her arms and hold her and there, in those arms of love, was the only place Meilin felt peaceful. For a moment she was safe. For a moment she was warm. For a moment the hunger did not hurt so badly.

Meilin found there were other children who were trying to find food. She learned to steal what she could, but the others were bigger and faster. Some were nice to her but many were mean and would hit her and take the food she found. One day she was caught trying to steal a vegetable from a merchant's cart. The merchant grabbed her by her skinny arm and would not let go.

The merchant took Meilin to a home where children without parents were kept. It was a meager existence, but she was given food to eat. The food was ugly and tasteless, but she was able to eat until she was full. It was the first time in a long time. That night, like so many before it, Meilin remembered her mother who tried so hard to feed her. Meilin cried herself to sleep.

There was a woman who would come to the orphanage and sit in their courtyard. The people who ran the home seemed to know her. The other children called her "the monk." One day Meilin approached the woman and asked her what a monk was. The woman explained that a monk was someone whose life was about helping others. "But what do you do?" Meilin asked. The woman laughed and pulled the little girl onto her lap and told her about giving things away. "I don't understand," Meilin said. "You don't have anything. How can you give things away?"

"I can give away smiles. Can you?" the woman asked her. As Meilin looked into the kind smile of the monk, she felt like she was back in her mother's arms. She let the monk hold her and speak gentle words of assurance her mother often spoke to her. For the first time since the awful day her mother died, little Meilin felt peace.

The monk, who was called Lian, became an important presence in Meilin's life. She learned it was okay to share the monk's hugs with the other children who came to her. She treasured the story times when Lian would tell tales of wise and foolish people and after each story remind the children that to let more into their lives, they had to give something away. The greatest gift, the monk reminded them again and again, was to give an act of kindness.

Those lessons from the monk became what filled the other hunger Meilin carried. Once she was able to get food for her body, Meilin craved her experience of the monk's hugs. She missed her mother's love and the tender care from Lian helped her to feel like her world was okay. With those needs fulfilled, a new need began to express itself in the young girl. Meilin's desire to understand the world had awakened; the monk's stories began to feed this newly awakened part of her being.

Meilin and several of the other children began visiting the home where Lian lived with other monks. Some were men and some were women. The children began to learn many things in the classes the monks taught.

Always at the core of their learning was the understanding of the power they had to make a choice. The choice was not an outer one. The choice that the monks spoke of was an inner one. To the children it became known as "the monk's choice." The monks explained to the children that this was the choice of moving their attention to their heart and drawing on a greater level of wisdom. They told the children that in their hearts they entered a realm of wisdom. In their hearts they would find a goodness that would help them meet the challenges of their lives. It was a choice they encouraged the children to try again and again.

As part of learning to activate her heart through making the monk's choice, Meilin learned how to fill her being with the flow of feelings of love. In those experiences she found a deep peace she had not known was possible. Even though her busy mind always seemed to be full of questions and ideas, this experience of filling herself with love awakened a deep quiet and peace within her. She found she loved the peace as much as she enjoyed the thoughts and ideas that seemed to want to overflow her young mind.

CHAPTER 16
GIVING

After Chen and her mother left, Meilin spent most of the afternoon sitting in silence. She watched the people of the town as they passed through the open area by the well. As she saw their slow gait, lacking the energy that good food and health provides, she once again remembered the beauty of the bird song. She remembered the smile of Chen, whose curiosity led her to speak to the monk. Her heart opened to feel compassion for these people caught in the midst of a cycle of nature that brought them the constant pang of hunger.

As she felt compassion, it brought a feeling of fullness to her heart. It was different from the feeling brought by the memory of the bird song. Rather it was the fullness that a mother feels for her child as she enfolds it in her arms. Meilin quietly breathed that feeling into the cells of her body and out into the simple village. She sent it out as a silent blessing of compassion and love to the people. With that full heart, she looked around her.

The monk found that she enjoyed the bright red color of the women's dresses. She appreciated the vibrancy and the feeling of hope it brought. She appreciated the hope that the people were trying so desperately to hang on to even as the reasons for hope seemed to have disappeared.

That evening Chen and her mother returned to the well to draw water. They again spoke to the monk and offered to draw water for her. The mother had been deeply touched by the monk's kindness to her daughter and to all the people of their village. She told the monk she would like to have her eat with their family that evening. She shared that they only had a few grains, some roots her husband had foraged in the mountains, and a small amount of goat's milk. She was embarrassed to offer so little, and yet it seemed to her like a very brave act to share it with another person.

Meilin responded with gratitude for the invitation. She joined the family that evening and participated in their meager meal. She knew that giving was a powerful act that dissolves barriers, and so she supported the family's generosity by participating in their meal.

As they talked that evening, the father talked of going farther away in search of food when he headed out in the morning. As the monk listened, she made an inner choice. With the family's anguish from their hunger all around her, she realized the importance of making the monk's choice.

She put her hand to her heart and focused on her feelings there. She began with her feelings of love and compassion for this young family. She felt her compassion for the father and mother, and she felt their great love for their little girl. As she rested in her heart, she found herself aware of the beautiful color of the clothing Chen and Nuo wore, as did the women of the village. She also vividly remembered the drab clothes of the women at the market in the village she had passed through days ago. Their clothing was dull, but their market was filled with the beautiful colors of their abundant vegetables. As these pictures filled her mind, the monk smiled with gratitude for the understanding they carried. When her spirit-self spoke to her through her heart, it always brought the understanding of the images it shared.

Meilin told the family how interesting it was to her; the contrast between the women in the drab clothing who had an abundance of meats and vegetables, and this village, so in need of food, yet filled with the clothing of beautiful colors the people made from the local bush.

She asked the father if he was able to travel the greater distance to the village she remembered and bring some of the beautiful material from his village. She asked him if he thought he could possibly trade the fabric for food.

There was a long silence at the table as the father and mother began to grasp the idea the monk had shared from her heart. Then a smile and excitement burst forth as hope touched the family.

The next day the monk returned to her fast. She understood that the villagers fasted from lack, yet she could join them and fast by choice. They saw that Meilin did not ask for food and that she, too, went without. Although they did not understand her fast, they knew she understood their hunger.

Several days later the monk was walking by the gate of the town in the late afternoon when she saw a wagon approaching. It was piled high with vegetables, grain, and other food. Leading the wagon was Chen's father. As he approached the village square, the people began to line up as the beautiful vegetables went from the wagon to their hands to their tables to feed their families. He told about the people in the distant town. He said they paid well for the beautiful cloth and clothing he had taken at his wife's bidding to sell in their market. He talked of their market overflowing with meat and produce and his having enough money from the sale of their beautiful red cloth to buy all the food he could bring home. That evening the monk was invited again to Chen's family home to join them for their dinner meal, which had enough for all of them to eat their fill.

The next day, several carts of beautiful clothing left for the distant town. The children were excitedly playing nearby as the wagons departed.

Meilin joined some of the women as they hiked into the hills above the village to pick more of the berries and resin used to dye the cloth. There was a different feeling, a new energy that filled everyone as they searched for the bushes. Meilin realized it was the energy of hope. Finally, there was a way to care for their families. It was as though the sun had come out after a long hard winter. Meilin enjoyed the feeling and treasured the first laughter that she had heard since entering the village.

The women worked with the dye and the additional plain cloth the men brought back with the food from the distant village. As Meilin helped the women, she shared the stories that she had treasured hearing from the monk, Lian, when she was a little girl.

After one of her favorite giving stories, she asked Chen, "What is your giving story?"

Chen responded by telling how she had given her friend the pretty stone and that she had given Meilin a drink of water. "Do you remember the givings that followed?" Meilin asked. Then she pointed out how Chen had given Meilin kindness and honesty when she had shared about being hungry. Her mother had given generously of their food when they had very little. She shared how an idea of the cloth for food had been given by spirit in response. She spoke of Nuo giving of her clothing and Chen's father giving of his strength and time to take the carts and giving freely to the others in the village when he returned with food. "This was a village of hunger. Now it is a village of generosity. That is in part because you gave," she pointed out to Chen.

The newly dyed cloth and clothing filled several carts as the men set out for the distant village. The men planned to return this time with some goats and perhaps sheep. Meilin watched the carts leave with her heart filled to overflowing with peace and fulfillment.

Feeling that peace, she understood that the wisdom that had guided her to this simple town was now calling her to go forward again. Meilin also departed that morning, but in a different direction. The monk waved good-bye to Chen as she headed down the path. From this village of generosity, she peacefully journeyed on.

PART 2B
TODAY

CHAPTER 17
THE MONK'S ROLE

Meilin's story is inspiring to me because she helped hungy people find relief. It stays with me because it suggests that in my own struggles, both inner and outer, there is a way I can find relief. Both of these results come from Meilin's choice, the monk's choice, the choice to connect with one's heart.

The story holds the monk's choice out to us as a powerful and transformative connection. The monk's heart is what gives her wisdom. It is what lifts her out of conflict and into peace. It is what lets our monk find joy amid lack and lift those around her to find their abundance. The monk's heart is a doorway, a portal to her spiritual self. In her spiritual heart is power. In her spiritual heart is wisdom. In her spiritual heart is the great meaning that comes from a higher perspective.

The monk's choice is how we, you and I, can connect with our spiritual natures. We have a physical nature, an emotional nature, a mental nature, and a spiritual nature. We live in our physical, mental, and emotional natures most of the time because that is how we are designed. Our brains access these natures quickly and directly.

Our spiritual nature is much older and wiser than what we accumulate in our physical experiences. The story depicts the invitation to choose our hearts, through which we connect with our spiritual nature. More specifically, it is the story of how we connect with our spiritual hearts.

Your spiritual heart is the core spiritual love, power, and wisdom that you are. It is your spiritual self as love, expressing for you and showing up in your experience. You experience it as transformative energy that moves you out of conflict and into peace, out of reaction and into direction.

Let's look at what the stories tell us when the monk makes the shift to the heart. The monk enters a village, and within that village there will be people who are experiencing a challenge. This challenge may be a form of lack, such as being without enough food, as it was for Meilin. It could also have been struggles with relationships in which people are misunderstanding each other, acting out their pain on each other, or projecting their fears on another. In Ming's story it was fear. triggered by not having water, a necessary element for life.

In the monks' stories every village the monk visits has a challenge because in our lives there is always challenge. Every part of life we experience has some sort of challenge for us to step into. I believe the monk, and the part of us she symbolizes, is growing in her journey just as we are. When the challenging stimulus comes before her, as for each of us, the choice is available to respond from the head or the heart.

When the monk makes the conscious choice of her heart, she releases herself from the emotional pressure of the challenge. The wisdom on how to respond in a way that is highest for her and for all who are involved is then available to her. The amazing surge of expanded consciousness within her is right there in that moment. It not only brings answers, it lifts her into the greater consciousness from which those answers can be successfully expressed.

This is the monk's choice in each village. This can be our choice in each situation we enter in our lives. Will we choose the heart? Will we bring our hand to our hearts and touch, then breathe? This is the choice before us. If we do, then we can take the step of engaging our heart feelings to connect with our spiritual selves. We then have the power to transform our worry and anxiety into peace.

Your spiritual heart has the wisdom to guide you through each step to a successful resolution. It lifts the consciousness of your being so that you respond from the place of honesty, clarity, compassion, or whatever your spirit is giving you as the path of transformation for that moment. When you are filled with that consciousness, you are changed in a powerful way.

What happens within us when we make the monk's choice? The identifiable changes are emotional balance, feeling good, wisdom, a new consciousness, and peace.

We have discovered that the monk's choice of the heart changes our bodies from the way we normally operate when our brains guide our perception and decisions. This physical change caused by the heart facilitates our connection to our spiritual nature. By activating the heart feelings in the second step of the Heart Wisdom Tool, we draw our spiritual energy into and through our hearts. Our hearts change their biophysical pattern into one that expresses greater wholeness.

This pattern of wholeness is identifiable in our hearts when we measure it. (Figure 18B, below) This pattern transforms our emotional response through its impact on the brain. This same pattern also enhances our brain's cognitive functioning.

The power of our spirit also lifts our perceptions by enhancing our intuition — the natural spiritual connection we have with everyone. We are filled with new power, in touch with new purpose. We arrive at a place of inner peace.

CHAPTER 18

COHERENCE & ENTRAINMENT

Today's scientific breakthroughs bring us a whole new perspective on what is really taking place during the time we spend focused on positive, energizing, love-related feelings in our hearts. Having a background in spiritual and religious traditions, I knew of the inspired ideas that love uplifts us, that love transforms us, and that love is the answer. These messages exist in different forms throughout spiritual and religious literature from almost all the major religions and teachers. They always felt like valid ideas to me.

And ... I realized early on in my role as a minister that those nice ideas were difficult to quantify and even more difficult to actualize in one's life.

I remember an experience that took place before I learned how to make the monk's choice. It was a situation where a woman in my organization criticized something I had done. It was not a major incident, just someone being critical. Even though it was minor, I felt hurt and defensive. I thought, *She really is wrong, and besides she would not have handled the situation as well as I did.*

My negative feelings and their attendant "thought loop" continued to haunt me for days. I thought about applying love and forgiveness; however, I did not know how to switch to love or forgive when I was feeling hurt. Making that shift was an idea I could not actualize.

Perhaps the ideal of the monk's story impacted me because I wanted to be able to live free of resentment. I wanted to be able to set down the burden of the resentments I frequently carried.

I observed that if someone got angry at the people I knew, they went into defense or attack. It just happened naturally. The idea of choosing love in a situation in which we feel hurt seemed ideally desirable and practically impossible. It was also true for me. It just seemed to me that I was controlled by the hard-wired response mechanism built into us all.

That's why I was so excited when I found that a different story was being told in the science lab. Research was showing that it was possible to choose something other than the standard negative emotional reactions when attacked or criticized. Within a short time of someone being negative toward them, some people were able to intentionally choose the love-related feelings of the heart. As I explored the research, it appeared that it was not that difficult to make this choice, once the person learned how.

It wasn't that the negative reaction did not occur; it did. However, once the individual became aware of his or her own negative reaction, another choice became possible: the monk's choice.

The research shows that when we make the choice to take the steps that lead to choosing love-related feelings, those feelings are the code that activates powerful biophysical changes. These changes are so profound they could be described as literally transforming our bodies. The transformation can be clearly monitored at the physical level of response. It can be monitored at the emotional level of response. And it can also be monitored at the cognitive level of response.

This transformation changes our bodies so that they now support us in experiencing the feelings of care and compassion.

With our changed bodies supporting our heart feelings, we are able to enter into a deeper connection with each other that is measurable.

Let me show you what that biophysical transformation looks like on scientific instruments.

The shift we are measuring in the following graph is from a negative feeling, such as frustration, to a positive one, such as appreciation. This shift, when sincerely felt, causes our heart patterns to transform. The specific heart pattern that it shifts is called Heart Rate Variability (HRV).

Heart Rate Variability measures the speeding-up and slowing-down of our hearts. Our hearts are always changing the speed at which heartbeats take place. Some beats are faster, such as when we are running, and some are slower, such as when we are sitting still. Even if we are sitting still, changes in our heartbeat speed still happen with every beat. Heart Rate Variability can be measured and graphed so that we can view its pattern. When we look at it captured on a graph, it is usually a fairly chaotic and disordered pattern, such as this one below:

Heart Rhythm Patterns (Heart Rate Variability)

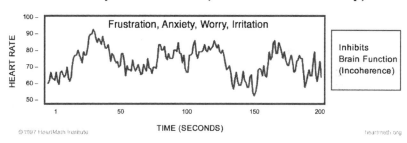

Figure 18A Heart Rate Variability — Frustration

This is the HRV pattern of a person sitting in a chair in the science lab at the HeartMath Institute in the Santa Cruz Mountains of California. When the line is going up, that means the person's heartbeats are speeding up. When the line is going down, that means the person's heartbeats are slowing down.

In this moment, the scientist asked the person to remember a moment when he or she felt frustration.

As you can see, there is no order to the pattern. It is chaotic. It is what scientists call incoherent.

An incoherent pattern similar to this is the pattern being generated by our hearts in most of our daily activities.

The next graph is the same person, still sitting in the chair at the research lab at the HeartMath Institute. Now the person has chosen to remember a moment of appreciation and is actively experiencing that feeling.

Heart Rhythm Patterns (Heart Rate Variability)

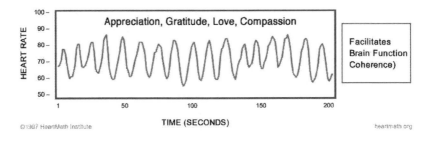

Figure 18B Heart Rate Variability — Appreciation

This pattern is not chaotic. It is not disorganized nor incoherent. This pattern shows great order or, in the scientific term, it is coherent.

Sitting in that chair and making the choice to remember a moment of appreciation and focusing on that feeling changed this pattern radically. It changed the way the person's heart was speeding up and slowing down from a disordered pattern to a highly ordered, coherent pattern.

Heart Rhythm Patterns (Heart Rate Variability)

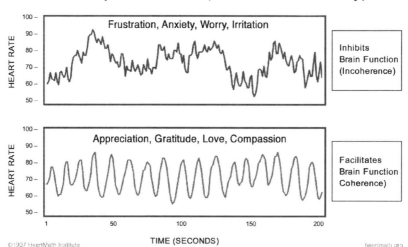

Figure 18C Heart Rate Variability — Transformation

This is a physical transformation. It is a change from one level of functioning to a higher level of functioning. When the scientists examined this shift from an incoherent HRV pattern to a coherent one, they discovered it also brings about major changes in other important systems.

The coherent pattern, this ordered speeding up, then slowing down of your heart, impacts your body in a dynamic fashion. It sends this same coherent pattern to the brain and causes major changes with brain functions.

It impacts a part of the brain called the amygdala, which selects our emotional reaction of frustration, fear, or anger. The ordered pattern from the heart changes how the cells of the amygdala pulse. It shifts the amygdala into an ordered pulse. The result is a shift in our emotional experience. We go from that a state of frustration, fear, or anger into a balanced emotional state. We are able to feel good where a moment before we were experiencing a negative emotion. This is a change that can happen very quickly.

Remember the last time someone was angry with you. Can you remember the feelings you had? Not the thoughts – the idea of how wrong or stupid or unsympathetic that person was. Remember instead the feelings, the possible feelings of anger, hurt, fear, rejection, or the pain of embarrassment. Remember how uncomfortable those feelings were and how long they stayed with you. Was it an hour? Were you still fretting about it later that day, that night, or the next day?

Would you like to be able to change your system to be free of carrying these types of feelings around? If you had known about it, you could have used the Heart Wisdom Tool to change that pattern in just a few minutes. Imagine feeling free of someone's verbal abuse in just a few minutes — feeling free, not burdened. That freedom from the control of the negative emotional reaction is the result of the heart causing a shift in the amygdala.

The second step of The Heart Wisdom Tool, Remember and Feel, activates this change in the HRV pattern of your heart. By impacting your amygdala, this change results in the ability to enter a balanced positive feeling and sustain that feeling. Your body changes from supporting the negative emotional reaction to supporting your positive feeling experience.

The change of your heart's HRV pattern from an incoherent to a coherent pattern also impacts a part of your brain called the thalamus. Your thalamus affects how you think and remember. The thalamus functions like a distribution center from which emanates the impulses that carry the data our brains receive across the cortex so we can identify and understand the stimuli around us. It has a core influence on our thinking capacity.

When the HRV pattern becomes coherent, the thalamus pulses that carry data across our brains become more ordered. As a result, your cortical functions become more efficient. The scientists call that "cortical facilitation." It basically means that you get smarter.

The heart's ordered HRV pattern affects our brain wave patterns. There is a syncing-up or "entrainment" between your brain wave patterns and your HRV pattern. Your brain and your heart become in sync with each other. I've often wondered if this isn't the biological reflection of personal integrity — a person operating with their brain and their heart in sync with each other. Having our core values and our thoughts in agreement feels like personal integrity to me.

This phenomenon of systems syncing up with each other, such as the heart and brain, is known as entrainment. It is the same type of phenomenon we see in schools of fish or flocks of birds moving in harmony. There can only be entrainment within an ordered system. A greater biophysical efficiency of our systems working together harmoniously is available when one's heart is in a coherent state. When our systems entrain with our hearts, we experience renewal and revitalization.

CHAPTER 19
HEART LOCK-IN

In the monks' stories, both Ming and Meilin have the skill to make the choice of their hearts and activate their hearts' power. We explored how we, too, can activate our hearts by using the Heart Wisdom Tool.

Both monks demonstrated a very powerful relationship with their hearts. They used their hearts to transform worries or challenges. They also used their hearts to maintain feelings of peace and to renew and revitalize themselves. Qualities such as emotional balance, resilience, and renewal are the result of having developed a strong relationship with their hearts. In a personal relationship, a strong relationship is one in which two people get to know each other well and communicate regularly, honestly, and deeply. It is the same with our relationship with our hearts.

It is helpful to spend time with the heart and its feelings to create a strong relationship with it. It is helpful to recognize what it feels like when you are in your heart, to know the feelings that are a part of your heart, and how your heart responds when you activate it and ask for its wisdom.

I have had the privilege of knowing many people who have sought to develop a close relationship with their hearts, similar to the one the monks' stories portray. I have observed that when these people meet challenges, they find it an easy and natural response to connect with their hearts.

They quickly "touch and breathe" and then move easily to remembering a heart-filled moment. They naturally find feelings, such as compassion. They report they can choose, in many situations, to feel appreciation or joy.

Many of the people I know who have made the effort to strengthen their connections with their hearts use a simple and very effective practice on a regular basis in their lives.

I think of this practice as spending a few moments in the monastery. It consists of simply spending a few minutes intentionally with my heart. My favorite way to do this is to use a technique developed by HeartMath that they call Heart Lock-In®. It consists of taking a few minutes to lock your attention in your heart.

I find it most helpful to do this simple exercise in a quiet space. The quiet space lets me concentrate without being distracted from the feelings I am activating. I enjoy sitting in a comfortable chair, usually in the mornings before my home becomes filled with activity. I close my eyes so I can focus all my attention on the inner feelings I will be activating.

As I describe these simple steps, I invite you to experiment with each one and see how it feels for you.

I begin my Heart Lock-In® by focusing my attention on the area around my heart. I like to touch my heart to draw my attention there. I take long deep breaths, imagining that the air is flowing in and out though my heart.

The second step is to generate a heart feeling. Just as with the Heart Wisdom Tool, I usually begin by choosing a heart-filled memory to activate my heart feelings. I might remember a moment with my family when we rafted the Salmon River rapids in Idaho, laughing with joy at the exhilaration of sharing that delightful adventure together. Sometimes my heart memory is of sharing a meal with friends, a special moment of connection or tenderness with my wife, Kathryn, or playing with my grandchildren and hearing their laughter. As I experience the sensation of my heart becoming full from the feelings in the special memory, I focus on experiencing those feelings.

For a few minutes, sometimes three minutes, sometimes five minutes, and sometimes fifteen or twenty minutes, I focus on feeling those feelings and their sensations as they fill my heart to overflowing.

Once those heart feelings are active, I notice how good it feels to be immersed in these beautiful feelings. I take a moment to consciously enjoy the goodness I am experiencing. Sometimes I explore shifting to other feelings that fill my heart with the delightful pleasure of positive energizing fullness. If I begin with a feeling of joy, I might shift into a feeling of care, appreciation, or compassion.

After I let myself focus on those heart feelings, I begin to radiate them out as if they were mighty currents of love power going out to bless the people in my life. I treasure the sensation of focusing my love, or other feelings that are a part of love, on the people I care about.

I send that love to my wife, to my children, to my grandchildren, to close friends, to the people I work with, to those I have made a commitment to hold in my prayers, to all those who come into my mind. This is a very uplifting experience for me. I'm not solving problems or fixing anything. I am just loving the people I love. I'm choosing to do it intentionally, consciously, and with great enjoyment. In radiating my feelings to those I care about, I have at times remembered Meilin's time of radiating her love and compassion to the villagers in their hunger.

Having radiated my positive feelings to others for several minutes, I redirect those feelings into a focus of love for myself. I feel the love that is present for me in that moment. I let it in and soak in that feeling. It seems to fill the cells of my body. I let it fill my feeling world. It fills me up until those delightful feelings become so great they want to overflow from my being.

This step – radiating the feeling of love to others and to myself – is energizing and uplifting. It gives me energy to get up and embrace a new day. It gives me energy to get going on what is important and meaningful for me. It fills me with joy, compassion, and peace.

When I open my eyes and bring my attention back into the room I'm sitting in, I let myself rest for a moment, enjoying the wonderful feelings that are a part of my life at that moment, enjoying the feeling of love in my heart. That is the way I use HeartMath's Heart Lock-In technique.

I lifts me and gives me energy. However, the real reason I'm sharing this with you is that I know this practice helps me in those places — those villages of my life — where I need to find my compassion. Like the monks, I find it possible to remember to choose my heart because I have spent time in my heart using Heart Lock-In®.

I know for Peter as well as for myself, Heart Lock-Ins make it easier to find our hearts when we are in our villages of challenge. It becomes easier to remember to use our Heart Wisdom Tool. It is easier to find compassion for someone else's fear because we previously had spent a few moments resting in the love and compassion of our hearts.

These are the two great tools that the monk's story is about for me. In whatever village I am in, when challenge arises, I can make the monk's choice. I can choose my heart by using the Heart Wisdom Tool to take me to my compassion. I keep strengthening my relationship to my heart by spending a little bit of time each day in my Heart-Lock-in so that when I want to choose my heart, it is familiar and inviting.

Because of my years with the HeartMath Institute, I often add to my Heart-Lock-in some background music from a CD called *Quiet Joy* that Doc Childre, HeartMath's founder, created to support the journey into our hearts. With his many years of working with the heart and guiding others through their heart experiences, he has a unique understanding of the energies and dynamics of our hearts. He created *Quiet Joy* to be a musical facilitator to our intention to connect deeply with our hearts.

In my Heart Lock-in I do not focus on the music. It simply supports me in the background as I focus on the beautiful feelings of my heart.

CHAPTER 20
THE MONK'S LIFE

The monk's story has always encouraged me that if I make the monk's choice, the choice of the heart, I open the possibility that I can be a beneficial presence to the villages I enter. This choice also helps me feel better in whatever situation I find myself. Our experience of life can become renewing and energizing because we can make the monk's choice, the choice of the heart.

What if you could meet your challenges from a place of feeling good, of feeling peaceful? You have the power to access this quality any time you notice you aren't feeling good. You can take a few minutes to access your heart and then return to enjoying your day regardless of what the villagers around you are doing.

The ability to walk through my life at peace is very important to me. I'm eager to respond to life's challenges that are mine to take care of and just as eager to get out of the way of the challenges that are someone else's to take care of.

I'm sure you have experienced both care and conflict in your life, tragedy as well as triumph. Perhaps you also have a desire to find out how you can find peace in the midst of your world — not after, but right in the midst of life's turmoil.

One of the most meaningful results of the monk's choice for me is the ability to access the deep wisdom of my spiritual heart right in the moment. I know that choice is always available in my experiences of conflict and when someone I love needs support. In these moments, the ability to access my deepest wisdom means the world to me.

I'm guessing our lives are similar, in that you find many decisions calling for your attention. Some are large and some small. However, all decisions affect others and make a difference. I am so grateful to know how to take the steps to access the deepest wisdom of my heart. I can't say I do it all the time. In fact, I often forget or just am so involved in a situation I don't remember the possibility of my spiritual heart's wisdom until afterward. However, when I do make that choice, even hours or days after the event, it makes a difference.

What a relief it is to know that you can reach deeper when a situation's path to resolution isn't clear. You can connect with that place in you where there is an answer. You can make a difference when your wisdom is needed.

Let's focus for a moment on what it is our monks, Ming and Meilin, may have learned or practiced so that they were ready to enter the villages and connect with their hearts regardless of what they might encounter.

First, each monk in our stories was committed to using a practice similar to the Heart Wisdom Tool when challenge arose in their world. I don't know if the monks were committed to using it in good moments as well. I find it pleasurable, and often helpful, to add more heart to any experience, even the pleasant ones, by using it frequently.

Part of the role we associate with a monk is regularly practicing specific disciplines or skills. Using a technique like the Heart Wisdom Tool to respond to the challenges of life is what I imagine might be a core spiritual practice of our monks. It is a technique that lets the monk stay true to his or her inner direction and not be pulled into the conflicts or fears of those around them.

In the story of the Village of Hunger, the monk shows us a second core practice that is at the center of her ability to choose her heart. It is the practice in which she fills herself with love and sends it out. That is similar to the practice the HeartMath people call Heart Lock-In.

It has been my experience that the more I use Heart Lock-In, the more my relationship with my heart grows. People have shared with me that when they consistently spend time in their Heart Lock-In, it gets easier to connect with their heart. Many people have also reported to me that during times when they have fallen away from taking the time for this simple practice, they find it more challenging to remember to choose their heart connection.

The Heart Lock-In is one of the easiest exercises to practice regularly and it can become one of the nicest, most enjoyable ways to spend your part of your day. When you are experiencing Heart Lock-In, you are enjoying the feelings of love, joy, and peace. You are in a state of compassion with the world and you feel good; actually, you feel great! To set myself up for feeling good all day – this is something that works for me.

The third thing I believe would be a part of the monk's path is to commit to using the Heart Wisdom Tool any time I don't feel good. In addition to using it when I'm challenged and using it when I'm having a pleasant moment, there are also times when there is no challenge except me. There are times when I'm not feeling good or goodness. I might just be in the blahhhhhs. Once my brain takes me there, it often does not want to let me go. I find if I touch my heart, I've already begun the journey to letting go of my head's negative feeling attachment and entering the process of releasing and letting myself go into my heart.

My commitment to using my Heart Wisdom Tool regularly, even if there isn't a challenge, has made a meaningful improvement in my life. I have also discovered that I need to cut myself a lot of slack and not judge myself when I don't remember to use it. I find sometimes I don't go to it right away, especially when I'm down in the blahhhhhs. I may even forget about using my heart until the evening.

Whenever I remember it, even hours or days after, I make the choice to use my Heart Wisdom Tool on the situation. I do it even if I can no longer affect the situation. What I can affect is my perception of it. I give my heart an opportunity to express its wisdom to free me from my unpleasant feeling. I get back into compassion and peace and can identify with my old friend the monk. Because of this commitment I find myself checking up on myself several times a day. Am I feeling peaceful or yucky? If the answer isn't peace, I know what to do.

The heart's gifts to the monk that we have looked at so far are:

1. Peace – the release of anxiety or replacing a reactionary experience with a feeling of peace. The peace may be filled with joy and fulfillment as much as serenity.

2. Wisdom – the ability to understand what is needed and how we can respond effectively. This clear direction saves us from much struggle and brings us harmony, as it did for Peter.

3. Vitality – a greater level of feeling good and an easier connection to the heart that comes from spending focused time enjoying our hearts, engaging our heart feelings, and radiating those feelings out to others and ourselves.

4. A spiritual connection — direct connection with our spiritual hearts creates an awareness that expresses as expanded consciousness. We are now looking at the situations in our lives with greater understanding people and often of the possibilities for a higher outcome. These more meaningful responses are not just for ourselves. They also support the higher potentials latent within the people and situations around us.

When I was young, I thought of the monk as so spiritual that he never got upset or hurt. I look at the story very differently now because I have seen so many people, even people with many years of dedication to their spiritual practice, enter their "village" and feel hurt or angry when unkind or unfair things are said or done. This happens in me as well. It's natural to have angry, defensive, or resentful feelings in response to the negative behavior of others. It was also a natural reaction for our monk to feel anger when the person from the village of fear told him he was not welcome.

Biologically, we are wired to react. The part of our brain called the amygdala filters all incoming data through our emotional database. If there is an emotional connection (it doesn't have to be an accurate match, just a connection), our amygdala triggers defensive reactions. The illustration I use in my workshops is of a person on a hike.

The hiker rounds a rock, sees a snake, and immediately jumps back. A moment later, the hiker realizes it is not a snake but a stick. The good news is that, if it were a snake and the snake was dangerous, the reaction might have saved the hiker's life. The person did not think, "That may be a poisonous snake so I should jump back to increase my chance of safety." If the person had taken the time to think that thought and it was a dangerous snake, it would probably have been too late. The instantaneous reaction is a built-in, emotionally charged defensive response mechanism.

Having been that person on a hike who jumped back in response to a stick, when I continued my walk I was constantly on the lookout for a snake. The reactive experience not only dominated that moment, it continued to influence my perception for some time after.

Knowing that our feelings of hurt, fear, or anger generated by our natural emotional reactions is a normal biological experience, I've seen many people use the monk's choice to move their internal response from feelings of hurt, fear, or anger to a feeling of compassion. They free themselves from the influence of that reaction. They get to hike on, enjoying the beauty around them instead of looking out for snakes.

When they do this, they often bring deep wisdom into their interactions with others. The dynamic of the monk's journey is not that the monk stays at peace all the time and doesn't change. Rather, it is that the monk keeps finding his or her way back to peace.

When the monk takes steps to transform his reactions so he can get to his feeling of peace, a creation of peace takes place around him. The monk leaves the village, having blessed it not only with wisdom but also with greater peace.

CHAPTER 21
ENVIRONMENTAL VILLAGE

Although it was many years ago, I clearly remember a moment of the expression of clarity and wisdom when I was in the role of a villager. Our "village" was an environmental regulation hearing in Santa Fe, New Mexico. The state environmental agency was suggesting a limit on some pollutant that was being emitted by a particular industry. The agency was holding hearings for everyone to give their input on the regulation. The hearing was very contentious, with many conflicting points of view.

At one point, the president of the Sierra Club, a participating environmental group, got up to speak. As an attorney for the state government. I was in the role of supporting the state agency that proposed the regulation and the state regulatory committee that was to adopt it. The environmental group had already submitted their testimony, so I wasn't sure why this man was approaching the microphone. Earlier, the industry representatives had been extremely antagonistic toward environmentalists, their leaders, and their point of view. I could well understand if this man had lashed out in anger in response to the condescending verbal attacks they experienced.

When the president of the environmental group began to speak, I realized that not only was he not angry, he was treating the experience with humor. He described the extreme views of his own group, the environmentalists, and their need to be so far out that a compromise would not put them in a losing position. He described how, after years of solid science about pollution harming people, the industry's representatives still claimed their toxic emissions didn't affect anyone. He described the state's attempt to find a compromise as missing a core issue that still remained to be settled. Having accurately and without animus described all the players, he then suggested a wise and effective way to approach the situation that clearly had merit as the best path to take.

I had been in many environmental hearings and I had heard a lot of positions and information. This was the first time I had ever heard true wisdom being offered. It affected everyone in the room and opened a way for that "village" to find its peace and effectiveness.

I did not realize it at the time, but that was one of my first experiences of finding a monk in the "village" of public regulation. Like the monk in the village of fear, this man had to overcome the negative things that were said about him and his group and his natural reactions to them. He had to find compassion for all the participants to understand their views. Like the monk who brought to awareness the solution of the beautiful cloth, he shared the wisdom that came from his heart. It was a broader, more inclusive perspective. You can do that, too.

You can enter your life situations, your villages, and even if you get triggered by fear, anger, or frustration, you can transform those feelings by choosing your heart and returning to your peace.

When we as individuals achieve a genuine feeling of inner peace, something is given to those around us. We are invited to a greater experience of peace, and we are guided on how to be a part of that creation, just as Peter was guided in how to respond effectively to Julia's needs. The monk's gifts are ours when we make the monk's choice.

CHAPTER 22
LINDA'S CHOICE

The amazing ability to set aside feelings of resentment and connect in a caring, constructive way with someone with whom we have conflict is another gift we get from making the monk's choice. In the past, when I've felt wronged, I tried to tell myself it didn't matter, or that the person didn't mean it, or that it wasn't personal. While at times such thoughts would reduce the intensity of my feelings, those thoughts from my head did not set me free from my feelings of resentment. When I discovered that our hearts have the power to release us from reactive emotions, I was able to successfully cease to carry the burden of resentment for another's past acts.

My friend Linda shared with me her experience in which she found old resentments awakening and she chose to use her heart. Linda's "village" was her greater family, both those in her household and her ex-husband. She brought forth such wisdom and release of resentment in that situation that I would like to share her experience with you.

Linda is the mother of Jimmy, who was four or five at the time. Jimmy has autism. This has presented unique and serious challenges to his mother. Linda and Jimmy's father divorced several years earlier, resulting in Jimmy's care being almost entirely in Linda's hands. Linda worked hard to help Jimmy successfully meet the unique challenges that autism presented.

One day Jimmy's father, James, called Linda and said that he had quit his job and he wanted more time with Jimmy. He wanted to go to half time in his relationship with his son. Linda was caught by surprise, even though she had been through similar experiences of James leaving jobs before. Those experiences had created chaos that was difficult for Jimmy to deal with, as plans and schedules changed. She had worked very hard to create a supportive and consistent schedule for Jimmy, something he needed to help overcome the challenges of autism.

Linda's initial response to James's call was anger. She realized that once more in this relationship it was about James and what worked for him. Even though she had explained it before, James was insensitive to how difficult it was for Jimmy to adjust again and again to two households, different people, and different expectations. James worked in the Florida construction industry and would change jobs several times a year. Linda knew from past experience that there would be another job for James soon. The schedule would then change again and Jimmy, for whom change was so difficult, would be asked to shift again because that was what worked for James. Linda had been down this road before, and her anger was easily justified. Linda was very aware of her feelings of anger as they grew. However, she decided to make a different choice. Linda made the effort to make the monk's choice.

Linda wanted to give James the reasons why his suggestion was selfish, insensitive, and would not work. She was legitimately frustrated that he did not realize, after all her hard work with Jimmy, how negative such a change would be to his son. However, before she said these things, she took the steps to make the monk's choice of choosing her heart.

When she took the steps to activate her heart, she could feel her spirit flowing through her heart. Her anger faded and she was filled with the clear understanding of how to respond to James. In response to her heart's guidance, she understood she could not work this out on the phone. She asked for some time to think it over and discuss it later. In spite of the frustrating situation before her, she was able to experience feelings of care for James, Jimmy, and herself

Later, when Linda met in person with James, she was able to share with James the options, the pluses and minuses, of the changes that his request would require in Jimmy's schedule. She asked James how he would suggest limiting the changes that upset Jimmy. She found herself not feeling judgmental but accepting and understanding, while still having the courage to share what she felt were the important considerations for Jimmy.

Linda's understanding of how she could connect with James in a way that would make it possible to work together to meet Jimmy's needs was the result of an expanded consciousness. With that greater awareness, she was able to see the potential of respect and cooperation that would let them really focus on Jimmy. An expanded consciousness is a gift from our spiritual hearts.

This greater view of the whole challenge, combined with the intuitive understanding of how to meet the needs of each person, was very different from Linda's original thoughts when she first heard James's request. As Linda followed her heart's wisdom, it led her step-by-step into this greater awareness and guided her successfully through her interactions with James.

Your spiritual heart will lift you into a new place of understanding. You can access it at any time. It is powerful enough to change your emotions, your thinking, and how you look at the situation before you. This is the core of your spiritual self, your spiritual heart. If you want to connect with a greater consciousness responding to your need, go to your heart and make the monk's choice.

Because Linda's experience is similar to many that can cause us frustration and easily escalate to conflict, let's look at it in greater detail.

In the initial call from James, Linda recognized her initial feelings of anger when they began within her. That is, in itself, a very significant accomplishment. Most of us get caught in an emotional reaction before we are aware that our defensive emotions have been triggered. Because she recognized her anger right away, Linda saved herself a lot of difficulty in dealing with James. Having recognized the angry feelings, Linda was able to use the skills she had learned to make the monk's choice, to go to her heart.

It was probably a very hurried version of the Heart Wisdom Tool. Because Linda had used it many times, it was natural for her to suddenly touch her heart and begin to take a deeper breath. Because of the pressure she was under, Linda probably did not take the full minute or two to deeply enter into her heart. Her use of the technique in that moment was more like a "mini" Heart Wisdom Tool. As she was taking that deeper breath, she most likely focused right away on the feeling that was a part of the memory she frequently used. That would have been easy because when we work with our hearts regularly, those feelings are close at hand. As she breathed into that feeling, her heart's wisdom would have naturally been more available to her.

With that wisdom showing her how the feelings of conflict could easily escalate, she received from her spiritual heart the idea of not trying to deal with the situation on the phone. She understood she needed to look much more deeply into her spiritual heart to know how to work with this issue successfully. She was able to say, "Let me think about what you have suggested, and I will get back to you." Her wisdom in that moment helped her overcome her angry reaction and handle the call effectively. Her head would have been focused on handling the issue, but her spiritual heart helped her see she only needed to handle the call from her ex in that moment.

Once Linda was off the call, she was able to focus more deeply on making the monk's choice. She intentionally connected with her heart with deeper feelings and sincerity than she had been able to during the call with James. Linda had worked with these heart tools for more than a year, so it felt natural to her to connect with her heart by touching and breathing. She went on to the second step of the Heart Wisdom Tool and recalled a heart-filled memory. She let the feeling from that memory fill her with its power. As she entered deeply into that feeling, the stress, anger, and tension from the call faded away.

Linda enjoyed experiencing the feelings as the memory she chose grew and strengthened within her. After spending a few minutes in that expanded place of feeling, Linda was able to sincerely ask her heart for a more effective response to James's request.

In response to her sincere asking, she realized she could bring all the concerns to him by engaging him personally in evaluating the problems for Jimmy. By doing this she could take his focus off what worked for him and refocus their discussion on what worked for Jimmy. In that way she could help James see the problem without having to reject his request directly, a response that in the past had made James angry.

Linda then got back to James and suggested that they get together to see what could work. Together they could review Jimmy's schedules that would be impacted.

Linda told me that because of her connection with her heart, when she met with James, she was not angry, defensive, or accusative. She had taken the time to do a Heart Lock-In before their meeting. She said she felt caring but also neutral. From that neutral place she was able to share the many questions involved in seeing that Jimmy received the care and consistency that he needed. She went over the pros and cons and asked for James's input.

As James's attention shifted to considering the extensive pattern of care that went into supporting Jimmy, James began to think differently about his request. At the end of their conversation he suggested that it would be best not to introduce more change into Jimmy's life. He suggested that because he was already looking for a new job they should leave the schedule the way it was.

Linda left feeling relieved that there would be no additional challenges for Jimmy. She left feeling successful in having communicated with her ex, something that had often been difficult. She also left with a strong connection with her heart and a clear awareness of the love and care that was guiding her thorough her life's challenges. She knew her spiritual heart's wisdom was always there, and she remembered again that it was accessible to her in a moment through making the monk's choice, the choice of her heart.

CHAPTER 23
INTUITION

Do you remember knowing something even though you didn't know how you knew it? That may have been an experience of your intuition. Perhaps it was an insight into one of your children or a close friend. Perhaps it was a sudden understanding about an important situation.

One of the powerful results of making the monk's choice is activating our intuitive capacity. Intuition is the ability to understand another person or situation at a deeper level than we achieve through our five senses. It allows our wisdom to not only be sensitive to our needs but also to the needs of those around us.

In the village where the monk experienced the villagers dealing with their fear caused by the dry well, Ming used his intuition to understand how to respond to the man who told him that he wasn't welcome in the village. The monk checked his inner response after making the choice of his heart. His inner response guided him to acknowledge the problem the men were facing and to share his recognition of how frightening the situation was. His intuition provided insight into an effective way for Ming to respond, which defused the villagers' hostile focus on him.

It was also the monk's intuition that brought to his awareness the source of water used for the crops and how this could provide for the villagers' needs. Ming's attention is drawn to the hillside where he notices the green of the crops near the spring. The awakening of a particular focus of attention (the green crops) is also a result of intuition. The meaning or potential in a situation (a source of water for the townspeople) is illumined by Ming's intuitive insight. Like Ming, our intuition gives us a greater awareness to the elements around us that are part of our solutions. We find that both our external and internal awareness is enhanced by our intuitive capacity.

In the village of hunger, Meilin's intuitive insight was about the value the red cloth would be to the people of another town that had an abundance of food. She realized its potential to provide for the hungry villagers' needs.

The monks' understanding of what to say, when to interact, when to be silent, and when to deliver their wisdom to the women, children, men, or community was the result of their intuitive insight. The expanded perspective let them be effective in bringing the care of their wisdom to the villages.

Peter's connection to his heart brought him an intuitive insight into how he could support Julia. He understood that holding her would help her move beyond the anxiety with which she was struggling. He also understood that he needed to be silent in that moment, so she could feel herself exercising her power of choice, instead of feeling powerless in her anxiety.

Linda's insight into how to respond to James was available to her after she made the choice of her heart. She was given very clear direction on a way to connect with him so they could explore the best option for Jimmy. That was not an easy thing to do because of Linda's frustration over the years with James' insensitivity to her and Jimmy's needs. The insight on how to deal effectively with Jimmy's needs in this situation by shifting James' focus from what worked for him to what would be helpful for Jimmy was very effective. This was something he was unlikely to do in their normal exchanges. However, her intuitive understanding of the value of this different focus opened the potential for James to tune into and respond to her need.

The response of our intuition is something that would have been understood simply as insight or spiritual guidance in the monks' time. Today we know that it is the result of specific changes activated by the change in our heart's Heart Rate Variability coherence pattern.

The heart generates an electromagnetic field, caused by the heart's electrical pulsing. This field is strong and clear enough that a person with the right equipment can detect its presence eight to ten feet from your body. This field contains waves or frequencies that emanate from the heart's electrical activity, like radio signals from a broadcasting tower. It's illustrated in Figure 23A.

The Heart's Magnetic Field

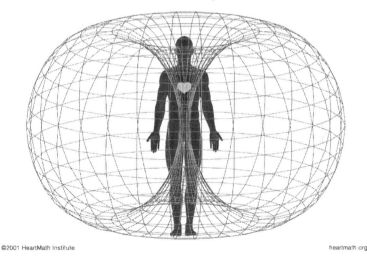

©2001 HeartMath Institute

heartmath.org

Figure 23A The Electromagnetic Field of the Heart

Some years ago, before the digital age, if you had a radio, you could turn the control knob and watch as the pointer passed across the screen from one frequency to another. Each frequency, indicated by a number on the radio dial, would correspond to a radio station sending out its content: pop music, oldies, country, news, and others.

When we analyze the range of frequencies the heart sends out, the graph looks like that old radio with vertical lines that represent the frequencies (one radio station after another) as we look from left to right.

In the science I'm going to share with you, we know that these frequencies, just like radio waves, can carry content, just like radio waves carry music or voices. Scientists have told me it is valid to think of the set of frequencies emanating from your heart as your intuitive field. It is through that electromagnetic structure of your heart that your intuition functions.

In step two of the Heart Wisdom Tool, remembering moments when our hearts were full, we activate the coherence pattern of our heart rate variability. This pattern affects the frequency structure that is generated by the pulsing of the electrical systems of our hearts.

If our hearts are incoherent, the frequencies are also incoherent. This incoherent set of frequencies creates what would be similar to static on the radio. If you try to send or receive content on that radio, you would hear mostly static.

However, the more coherent our hearts are, the more coherent the heart frequencies become. As these frequencies become clear and distinct, the message or content of thoughts and intentions are more easily carried on those frequencies.

The understandings we call intuition are carried by the electromagnetic frequencies of the heart. Figure 23B (below) shows the frequencies (the vertical lines) that are emanating from a person's heart.

In Figure 23B you can see how the incoherent frequencies on the right side look like static. Just as on a radio, it would be hard to receive the content carried by those frequency waves. The frequencies captured on the left side are clear and distinct. Those are the kind of wave structures that can carry a clear signal.

The way we activate the change from incoherent to coherent in the frequencies of our hearts is through the deep heart feelings similar to love, care, and compassion that we activate in our heart memories.

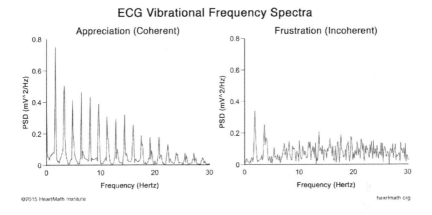

Figure 23B Heart Frequencies

In learning about intuition, I came across a fascinating experiment conducted by the HeartMath scientists. It dealt with the role of our heart's electromagnetic field in sending information from a person. The scientists wanted to know if we could impact something beyond ourselves by thought or intention. They were testing the hypothesis that the heart's electromagnetic field was the instrument that carries the thoughts or intentions.

To test this, they selected samples of DNA as the objects thoughts would be directed toward. DNA is stable at room temperature and its change (it winds or unwinds) is easily measured with a spectrometer.

They selected a person to focus his or her thoughts and intention on the DNA sample. The scientists had the person intend for the DNA to perform the specific change of winding. During the experiment the scientists were monitoring the coherence pattern of the person's heart.

When the subject intended by his or her thought for the DNA to wind, the DNA did wind. When I heard that, it was a "Wow!" for me. A person was able not only to influence but actually direct material outside of themselves simply by their thoughts and intentions. However, when the thought and intention were there, the DNA did not always wind. The DNA responded to the subject's intention for it to wind only when their heart pattern was in a coherent state.

When the person activated their heart's coherence by selecting heart feelings, the electromagnetic waves became coherent and able to carry the thoughts and intentions, impacting the DNA sample and resulting in the change desired.

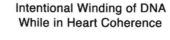

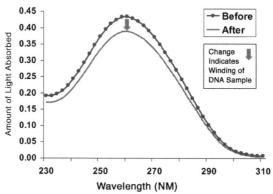

Figure 23C DNA Winding

The opposite intention was also tested. The subject was asked to intend the DNA to unwind while the subject's heart was monitored. In response to the person's intention, the DNA did unwind, but again, only when the person's HRV pattern was in a coherent state.

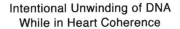

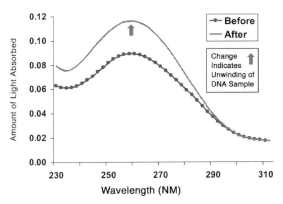

Ultraviolet Light Measurements from Spectrophotometer

©1993 HeartMath Institute   heartmath.org

Figure 23D DNA Unwinding

This experiment helps us understand that the electromagnetic field of the heart is an instrument through which our thoughts and intentions are radiated out from our persons and impact the world around us.

This may be why we ask certain people to hold us in prayer as we face sickness or challenge. We know their love will make a difference as their intention for our well-being impacts our bodies and our lives. Perhaps we intuitively feel the potential of their love creating a coherent heart field, carrying their sincere desire for wholeness to the cells of our bodies.

The above experiment had to do with sending information through our heart's electromagnetic field. Further research supports the understanding that we are also more receptive to receiving information intuitively when we are in heart coherence.

These discoveries helped me understand how the monks' choice of their hearts helped them intuitively know how to respond to the people of the villages. It also helps to explain the expanded perceptions they both had in recognizing solutions for the challenges the villagers were facing. Their hearts provided them with a greater intuitive capacity and insight.

I want to share another experiment with you that gives two powerful pieces of information. It established the receiving nature of our heart and its electromagnetic field. It also introduced information I interpret as strongly suggesting the interaction of our spiritual nature through our hearts.

This experiment was particularly intriguing for me because I was one of the test subjects.

The subjects were seated in front of a computer monitor. The researcher would push a button initiating a sequence of events. Six seconds after the button was pushed the computer would randomly select an image and display it on the monitor. The randomly selected images were either neutral, such as the image of a rock, or they were emotional images, such as a gun, coiled snake, or knife. Two-thirds of the images were neutral.

The subjects were wired up extensively, with sensors on our heads, hearts, and hands. The intention of the experiment was to see if there was any different response to the emotional images and, if so, when that response occurred.

The results surprised me. It turns out that if the computer was going to select a neutral image, no change in brain or heart preceded the image. However, if the computer was going to select an emotional image, after the button was pushed but 4.8 seconds before the computer selected the image, the heart responded and sent a signal to the brain. How did it know that the image would be an emotional image when the computer had not yet selected the image?

Not only did the heart receive information about something that was going to emotionally impact the subject, it knew the nature of that choice before the computer made a selection.

My interpretation of this result is that there is something that operates independent of time and space that connects us through our hearts with the world around us. This presence, which I call our spiritual nature, can sense emotional potential and communicate that challenge to the brain so we can be prepared to meet it.

How wonderful it is that our hearts constantly and intuitively assist us in responding to life and the world around us.

These experiments helped me understand what I have observed in individuals' experiences: the more coherent our heart frequency spectrum, the more clearly we are able to perceive the intention, needs, thoughts, or feelings of another. Coherence heightens our capacity to send clear intention. It also heightens our ability to receive and understand another's experience.

Because coherence is created by our heart feelings that are a part of love, we could also put it this way: Love heightens our capacity to send clear intention. Love also heightens our ability to receive and understand what another person is going through.

Parents know the experience of understanding a child's needs even though the child can't articulate them. The love and care within the family heightens the intuitive connection. My brother, sister, and I used to say my mother had eyes in the back of her head because she knew things that we thought we had cleverly hidden, kept secret, or disguised. In fact, she loved my sister, brother, and me very much and was therefore highly intuitive.

Let's look again at Peter's experience and explore his connection with his intuition. When Peter needed to connect with his wisdom, what he did was go through the set of steps that let him access his heart. His mind was struggling because he wanted to help Julia feel better. He wanted her to clearly see the choices before her and to have confidence that she would make the right decision. He knew that if she could get beyond her anxiety, she would be able to see her way clearly.

However, the anxiety caused stress for both of them. Peter's mind wanted, as our minds do, to answer the question, "How do I end the anxiety?" Peter's intuitive capacity was accessed when he made the monk's choice and connected with his spiritual heart.

Having activated his intuitive capacity, he recognized that words would overwhelm Julia. However, he understood intuitively that she would be receptive to his feelings of love and care, through being held. That intuitive capacity of his spiritual heart gave him the wisdom to ask Julia if she was open to being held. That easy invitation left the power in her control and invited her to enter a world that felt different from what she was feeling. It invited her into a world that felt care, love, warmth, and safety.

The scientific research has helped me understand the power and validity of the techniques I have been sharing with you. Objective measurements from the scientific research are helpful.

However, the activation of our hearts and its result are experienced subjectively. For that reason, I have also found that I learn, increase my understanding, and grow in my ability to choose my heart as I hear of other people's experiences in making this choice. Just as the monks' experiences helped me realize the potential in making the monk's choice, what other people have experienced in making that choice has been very instructive to me.

For that reason, I want to share with you a number of people's experiences in very different situations. I invite you to think of these people as monks who found themselves in a particular "village," with its unique challenge. The village may have been an organization, a personal relationship, a traumatic situation or simply the village of internal discord. They each chose to make the monk's choice to meet their challenge.

CHAPTER 24

STEVE AT CONVENTION

A good friend of mine who I'll call Steve had an opportunity to test the idea that the monk's choice lets a person access a greater intuitive wisdom that brings a solution to problems even when many other people are involved. The opportunity came to Steve when he was the chairperson of the governing board of a large religious organization. The organization's annual convention was about to be held, which included its annual meeting, where the group's business was conducted. He was responsible for conducting the meeting where at least five hundred people would be present.

He explained to me that throughout the year there was a person, let's call him Jay, who had been vehemently opposed to how a disciplinary process had been handled. The organization always sought to be responsive to its members' needs and had very thoroughly investigated the questions that Jay raised. The leadership, my friend included, were all satisfied that the outcomes were fair and just and that it would be disruptive and unfair to accede to Jay's demands.

As with any passionate person, Jay had rallied a number of his friends around his role of opponent. The number of people was not significant; however, Steve and others were deeply disappointed with the contentiousness of their resistance and the disruption their opposition brought to the organization.

As he approached the meeting, Steve told me he felt like the monk who had entered into a village of contention. He did not know if he could do anything about the situation. However, if there was a possibility of defusing the conflict, he wanted to make sure he tried to do what he could.

Before the meeting, Steve used the Heart Wisdom Tool and went to his heart. He told me that as his spiritual heart responded, he began to see the situation differently. He saw a group of people who were convinced they were right not because of the facts, but because they needed recognition and acknowledgement that their point of view was of importance.

Steve asked his spiritual heart if there was a way to defuse the situation. Was there a way that would acknowledge these people and yet not give in to their demands or undercut the ethics system that the organization's members adhered to?

His heart responded by giving him the understanding that if some of the concerns of both groups could be set aside, it would free everyone involved. He was guided to suggest to the board of trustees that a panel of independent individuals be chosen to look at the situation under specific guidelines that would not set aside what had been done but would ensure an impartial look at the fairness to those involved. At the convention he connected with Jay and asked him if the limited, independent review would acknowledge his point of view and feel fair. Jay accepted the idea and together they created a working framework.

At the opening of the business meeting, Steve acknowledged the concerns of members who were upset. He announced the formation of the independent limited review group and Jay, who had been so opposed to Steve and extremely critical of his leadership, stood with him in front of the conference body and acknowledged that this would be a fair way to address the concerns the group was upset about.

Steve said he walked away from that "village" feeling his spiritual heart let him bring a measure of peace that had been missing in the organization for some time.

The challenge for Steve was that he believed he and other members of the leadership were right and those criticizing the process were wrong and without basis. In fact, the leadership under Steve had been more than fair to all concerned. When Steve entered his heart and surrendered this position that his head claimed so strongly, he was shown there were other needs involved for the people who were complaining. It was only then that he understood that caring for the whole was as important as the position of being right. Intuitive wisdom from his spiritual heart showed him a simple way forward that would meet everyone's needs. The willingness to respond through that greater wisdom brought peace.

The monk's choice, the choice to activate one's heart, opens the intuitive awareness that is sensitive to an expanded perspective. For Linda, this expanded perspective was sensitivity to her ex-husband's needs. For Meilin, this expanded perspective included the needs of the hungry people in the town, combined with the awareness of the need for beauty in the town that had plenty of food. For Steve, it was the need for acknowledgement of Jay and his friends who were upset.

CHAPTER 25
CINDY'S CHOICE

One of the clearest examples to me of the capacity of our hearts to open this intuitive wisdom was shared with me after I conducted a large workshop where people practiced the Heart Wisdom Tool and applied it to situations in their lives.

A woman named Cindy, like Ming and Meilin, went through the steps of entering her heart and experiencing a clear shift of perception.

Cindy shared that she was very unhappy and depressed when she entered the workshop. She believed there was no hope for her marriage and that, even though she still loved her husband, their interchanges had become so filled with conflict that she needed to get a divorce. This was weighing heavily on her feelings. Cindy had examined her situation from many angles, and she did not see a way out of divorce as the solution. It was hopeless. Her marriage was soon to be over.

Cindy took a few minutes in the workshop to use a HeartMath technique very similar to the Heart Wisdom Tool. As I led her and the other participants through the steps of this technique, she applied it to her situation with her husband. The technique helped her make the same choice as the monk — it let her choose her heart.

Within a few minutes of applying the steps of the technique, Cindy was suddenly viewing her situation from a completely different perspective. With a deep intuitive insight, she understood the challenge that was triggering the reactions from husband and she understood how she could help him through it. This different way of perceiving the situation opened up a whole new set of responses for her. She could clearly see that these responses would solve the conflicts they were experiencing. She also recognized that this different way of responding would make their marriage stronger.

Cindy was thrilled! She was so excited that she shared the joy of her discovery with a friend she had come with. The friend called me over so Cindy could tell me about her experience.

Cindy told me she had been hearing words of criticism from her husband. She was justifiably hurt and angry. As this criticism continued over time, she became more hurt, depressed, and angry. She found herself both expressing that anger to him and burying some of the feelings inside her. She knew that neither was helping her marriage.

When Cindy connected with her heart, her perception of her husband changed. She didn't see him as angry and critical. Instead, she intuitively recognized that he had become afraid and insecure. She understood that difficulties he was facing at work resulted in his feeling out of control and vulnerable to events he did not have power over. Cindy realized that what he needed from her had nothing to do with the subjects of their conflicts. What he needed from her was validation that he was okay and that his thoughts and ideas were good.

Cindy realized she would love to give her husband validation. She saw the opportunity to respond by validating his ideas and giving him assurance of his value and importance. Her heart was full of joy and her eyes were filled with tears of joy. This was not about the ending of their marriage. This was an opportunity for her to support him as he was passing through a painful situation. She no longer felt anger toward him. She felt compassion, care, and love.

Cindy no longer felt turmoil about this relationship. She felt at peace. She was grateful that she did not need to be a part of frustration and conflict in their home. Now she could be a presence of care, wisdom, and love.

Cindy expressed her amazement to me at how clear her direction was and how deeply she understood the ways she could help her husband and their relationship. The vibrancy and joy I saw on her face was inspiring. She was radiant with the freedom and power that deep wisdom brings. Her world had changed because of the deep intuitive wisdom she accessed when she made the monk's choice.

CHAPTER 26
SUSAN'S CHOICE

I have a wonderful sister-in-law, Susan McArthur, who shared with me an experience of the monk's choice. It is really quite simple, and I have found it one of the easiest and most rewarding of the feelings that the monk can choose. That is the choice to feel appreciation.

Susan was driving down from a mountain ridge into the beautiful valley that contains Sedona, Arizona. This is a spectacular valley with rock formations that are stunning. There is a beautiful red color in the rocks of the cliffs and magnificent towering formations that fill the valley.

As Susan was returning from some days away for her job, she topped the rim of the canyon and began to drive the series of switchbacks that would bring her into the canyon and her home. She was eager to get home, tired from days of working and traveling, and was looking forward to rest, seeing her family, and a good night's sleep.

The Sedona area is a tourist destination because of its outstanding natural beauty. More than three million people visit Sedona each year. As Susan began to drive the switchbacks that let her reenter the valley, she had to come to a stop again and again as cars pulled off and on the highway. The tourists were stopping to look at the gorgeous view spread out before them. The time it took for them to pull over and take pictures and reenter the traffic really slowed everyone down. Susan found herself going very slowly; it seemed as if she would never get home. As one driver after another interrupted the flow of traffic, she became aware of her spiraling irritation and frustration. Her thoughts naturally focused on how stupid and inconsiderate these people were. It was tempting to think of them that way because it felt so justified.

However, realizing the discomfort of her own feelings, she chose to make the monk's choice. She took the time to direct her attention to her heart by touching and breathing.

As she entered the second step, Remember and Feel, her spiritual heart brought to her the memory of the first time she had entered this valley. She remembered how it took her breath away and how, just like the tourists, she stopped driving to take in the amazing panorama before her. As her heart responded to this memory, she was able to appreciate the people's excitement upon seeing the stunning beauty of the valley.

There was no problem to solve; the traffic would not move faster. This was simply a moment in which she exercised the power to change her internal "village" from frustration and resentment to a village of appreciation. The stress in her body dissipated. She was now slowly driving in a place of beauty, feeling appreciation and internal harmony. She was not in conflict. She was at peace. When she entered her home, she would be, just as she was on the highway, a presence of peace.

The power of our spiritual nature to flow through our hearts and put us in tune with what is around us is its own magnificent type of wisdom. Susan's experience was very simple and her shift of perception was very important to the quality of that moment. Being open to the quality of life around us has a great impact on the quality of life we experience. The only problem presented to Susan was how to deal with her own emotional reactions. The transforming power of making the monk's choice, of choosing her heart, took care of that problem.

Most of the examples I have shared with you were chal-lenges that involved responding to people who were known to me or known to the person who made the monk's choice. They were interacting with family, business associates, or just with internal questions of their own. I want to share with you one more experience because it was with someone I did not know. It involved a situation of great need that felt impossible and hopeless. In this situation, the solution that the spiritual heart could bring was limited. However, its response impacted the quality of the experience even though it could not impact the outcome. Like Susan's experience, it reminds me that the quality of life we experience has a greater potential when we use this wise transformative power of our hearts.

CHAPTER 27
HOSPITAL CHOICE

This experience occurred when I was a young minister. I was only two or three years out of seminary and had almost no experience dealing with people's pain and tragedy.

I received a phone call around two in the morning from the local hospital. The caller informed me that a person who had listed my church on their hospital information was now in the midst of a very difficult crisis. I did not know the family well, but got up and left right away for the hospital. When I got to the hospital, a tragic situation that had unfolded for a mother and her two sons was explained to me. The mother had already died and so had one of the little boys. The father was down the hall with the other little boy, who was also near death.

I arrived at the waiting room, to find some friends and family members gathered. I did not know them, but they were gracious in greeting me and allowing me to pray with them for God's love and healing.

The hospital staff member came in and invited me to go into the room with the father and his son. She explained that the little boy was only being kept alive by machines and they would be unplugging them soon.

I was about to step into a room to support a man I had met only briefly and whose family had suddenly been eliminated from his life. That morning he had a wife and two beautiful young sons. At this moment the last of the three people he loved most was about to be taken from him, from life itself.

I would step into that room with no idea of what to do. What could I say to a man who just experienced the death of his wife and son? He would be with his little boy whom he was about to release to death? I felt overwhelmed for him and felt my own tears rising in response to the depth of pain and loss before me.

I followed the nurse into the room and saw the father sitting beside the bed in which his son lay. The little boy was lying motionless with the tubes breathing for the child and keeping him alive. When I looked at the father my heart went out to this man. I felt such deep compassion for the unimaginable pain he was experiencing.

It was a natural response to feel compassion for this man whose life had suddenly shattered. I sensed his overwhelm and sense of powerlessness. I knew he loved his family and his heart must feel torn apart. I looked across this large hospital room at this father and saw him sitting helplessly beside his dying son's bed. In spite of his love for his child, there was nothing he could do.

Suddenly, as I felt my compassion, I experienced a greater awareness of the situation. I realized there was one thing this father could do. In this last minute of his son's life, my heart told me he could hold his child. There was no benefit for the child to be in the bed separate from his father. I turned to the nurse and asked if the child could be put in his father's arms so the father could hold his son as the child completed his life journey. The nurse seemed startled, and then a sense of recognition appeared on her face. She asked the medical personnel to help her and after asking the father if this was acceptable to him, they lifted the little boy into his father's arms.

This man whose family had disappeared in a moment had at least one moment to hold this beautiful little boy and touch him as his father. He got to enfold him in his protective arms – not arms that would protect him from death, but arms that would protect him in this last moment of life from loneliness, from separation.

I knew intellectually that the physical child may not have known the difference; however, I wasn't even sure of that. I did feel that this little boy would experience his father's love. The father held his son and cried. He rocked him in his arms.

Every heart in that room was touched by the father's love as he held the child in his arms and spoke his love to the little boy. We all knew this was special and important to both father and son.

We waited and held a sacred watch with the father that day. After a time, the medical staff asked the father if they could complete the release. The father understood, and continued to hold the child in his arms as the machines were unattached. The boy's journey in this life was completed.

When I had the opportunity to step back and reflect on this experience, I realized that something unexpected had happened for me. I had not known what to do. I had little knowledge about this family. Like the monk, I simply found myself in their village. My heart in its compassion had simply found a way to respond to a need and give voice to that way of response. The response was not from any training I had ever received, nor was it from my experience because I had little other than my own personal experiences of loss.

The monk's choice happened for me because my heart was opened by my compassion. An insight was given to me from my spiritual heart. Like the monk in the village where the well went dry, in that moment I was able to understand the situation from a broader perspective that included the intuitive understanding of the father's need and the potential that a greater possibility of connection would respond to that need.

The response to my insight changed that moment and the experience of everyone in that room. In that most difficult moment, that small change made a difference for the father and I do believe it made a difference for that little boy.

Even though at that time I did not yet understand the power of the sincere feeling of compassion, I activated the same access code – compassion — that guided the monk to help the villagers in their need.

That process, the monk's choice, connects us to the presence of a greater capacity within us. It accesses a greater understanding of what is unfolding in our world.

That day in the hospital, making that choice established a connection I would spend years exploring. It revealed a wisdom I have come to understand is available to us all in our spiritual hearts. It is the same wisdom that brought peace and greater understanding to the monks.

The monks' secret was that wherever they went, they knew how to access this wisdom through the power of love and compassion. This wisdom brought forth insights they needed to respond in a way that helped fulfill the needs of the people around them.

CHAPTER 28
TODAY'S MONK

Today, you are the monk. You have been learning how to make the monk's choice as you go on your own journey from village to village—from family to business to friendship and to causes you value. As you travel through experiences of challenge and conflict, one of the most important explorations will be learning to access this amazing wisdom that you, as the monk, bring to the villages you enter.

It is important to remember what wisdom is and what it is not. The simple wisdom to let the father hold the boy was an idea that fulfilled an important need. It did not heal the boy. It did not reverse the tragedy that had unfolded. It did add greater quality to the experience of the moment. It changed a moment from separation to connection, from love that was frustrated and blocked to love expressed. It let a child complete a journey in his father's arms instead of in a bed touched only by modern medicine's tubes and machines.

Wisdom's gift is that it lets us interact in each moment from the highest response within us. It brings connectedness. It brings the insight necessary to respond to our situations with a respect for each person. It doesn't pretend a person does not have the challenge that is theirs. What it does is lift our perception and fill us with insight to respond to challenges in ways that can lift the quality of the moment. The monk's choice of the heart lifts us from confusion to clarity, separation to connection, and powerlessness to effectiveness.

How can you make this choice, the monk's choice, the choice of your heart and its wisdom? The steps are easy.

1. Touch and Breathe

2. Remember and Feel

3. Sincerely Ask

As you enter the villages of your life, you are the monk. Enjoy the wisdom of your spiritual heart.

END

* * *

RESOURCES

Dear Reader,

If you would like more information about the wisdom of your heart, how to access it and use it, here are some resources that I hope you will find helpful.

My books about heart wisdom:
The Intelligent Heart, (ebook) by David McArthur and Bruce McArthur, describes the role of the heart and its wisdom in one's spiritual growth. It explains the universal laws, also called the spiritual laws, and highlights the experience of personal transformation. It includes extensive HeartMath research plus information on heart intelligence, and a number of HeartMath's techniques.

Your Spiritual Heart, by David McArthur, focuses on my journey of discovering the spiritual connection and the transformative spiritual power accessed through our hearts. It expands on the understanding of our spiritual or soul nature and its wisdom. It is designed to help deepen the experience of the Heart Wisdom Tool.

Books by HeartMath
The HeartMath Solution, by Doc Childre and Howard Martin, gives a broad overview of HeartMath's research, techniques and applications.

Transforming Stress, by Doc Childre and Deborah Rozman, is an excellent experience of HeartMath core techniques and their practical applications.

Heart Intelligence, by Doc Childre, Howard Martin, Deborah Rozman Ph.D. and Rollin McCraty Ph.D., focusses on heart wisdom from four of the people who understand it best.

Other Resources:
The HeartMath Experience is a video learning experience that is an excellent way to learn about HeartMath's discoveries and techniques.

The Connection Practice is an outstanding application of heart wisdom in the experience of communication. It is one of the finest methodologies for transforming conflict and difficult communications into heart connection and understanding. The above link gives access to information, trainings and books.

AccessingWisdom.com is my website which has information to trainings, classes and materials on heart wisdom and its applications. It is also a way to connect with me for speaking engagements and personal consultations.

David McArthur

ACKNOWLEDGEMENTS

My wonderful wife, Kathryn, is my support and constant inspiration for connecting with my heart. I'm so grateful that I listened to my heart's direction and asked her to share this life's journey with me.

Thank you to those who helped this book take form: Tom Bird and his excellent team, Lisa Nichols who made me look literate and my support team of Jessica Gallegos and Linda Curry. Thank you, Toni Roberts, for your heart's beautiful wisdom and friendship.

In the Santa Cruz Mountains there is a village of people who enhance humankind's knowledge of the heart and diligently live that knowledge to make it real. Thank you to our HeartMath family and especially Doc Childre who is gently awakening the world to its greatest potential.

My heart fills daily with gratitude for my family. My children Lisa, Peter and Anna, their spouses Alx, Julia and Chris and our delightful grandchildren Corwin, Fiona, Marlowe, Kirra and Reef all inspire me with their magnificent hearts.

ABOUT THE AUTHOR

Rev. David McArthur, J.D.

David McArthur's passion for understanding human transformation has taken him on a powerful journey into the discovery of the spiritual heart and how we access its wisdom. His desire to help others led him to an initial career as an attorney, working with environmental and consumer issues. His recognition of the power of our spiritual nature took him into spiritual study and ministry. He supported individuals and groups of people in personal transformation as a Unity minister for more than thirty-five years.

Seeking the scientific principles of transformation drew him to the HeartMath® Institute. He served on the HeartMath staff for seven years, including roles as a principle speaker and trainer as well as a director of their empowerment and religions divisions. There he discovered that through the choice of the heart, real moment-by-moment transformation and wisdom can deeply enhance everyday life.

David McArthur co-authored with his father *The Intelligent Heart*, with its revelation of heart intelligence. He then shared with us the source of that wisdom in *Your Spiritual Heart*. Now, having worked with thousands of people who have sought to make the choice of their hearts, he brings us *The Monk's Choice*. Here are inspiring stories, illustrating a scientifically tested, spiritually powered guide to accessing your deepest wisdom. *The Monk's Choice* brings to life the option to choose your heart. More at http://www.accessingwisdom.com.

Made in United States
Orlando, FL
18 March 2022

15901325R00096